BSCS Science Tracks

Connecting Science and Literacy

Investigating
Ecosystems

Second Edition

BSCS

KENDALL/HUNT PUBLISHING COMPANY
4050 Westmark Drive   Dubuque, Iowa 52002

BSCS Staff, Second Edition

BSCS Administrative Staff

Carlo Parravano, Chair, Board of Directors
Rodger W. Bybee, Executive Director
Janet Carlson Powell, Associate Director
Pamela Van Scotter, Center for Curriculum Development
Marcia M. Mitchell, Director of Finance

Project Staff

April Gardner, Deborah Jordan, Project Directors
Barbara Perrin, Director of Publications
Dottie Watkins, Production Coordinator
Stacey Luce, Manuscript Specialist, Permissions
Pamela S. Warren, Assistant to Center for Curriculum Development Director
Judy L. Rasmussen, Assistant to Center for Research and Evaluation Co-Director
Dave Somers, Colorado Springs, Colorado, Editor

Field-Test Teachers and Coordinators

Karen Abrams, Grade 4, Green Valley Elementary School, Denver, CO
Teri Appell, Grade 5, Southmoor Elementary School, Denver, CO
Deborah Baho, Grade 3, South Street Elementary School, Fitchburg, MA
Kim Bellio, Grade 3, Reingold Elementary School, Fitchburg, MA
Ellyn A. Bourque, Grade 3, South Street Elementary School, Fitchburg, MA
William Bourque, Grade 3, South Street Elementary School, Fitchburg, MA
Carrie Boyden, Grade 5, Memorial Intermediate, Fitchburg, MA
Sarah Brown, Grade 3, Harrington Elementary School, Denver, CO
Susan Buck, Grade 4, Steck Elementary School, Denver, CO

Kristy Collins, Grade 3, Southmoor Elementary School, Denver, CO
Kerri Cormier, Grade 4, Reingold Elementary School, Fitchburg, MA
Karen Croteau, Grade 4, South Street Elementary School, Fitchburg, MA
Stephanie Csikos, Grade 4, Park Hill Elementary School, Denver, CO
Amy Dessureau, Grade 4, Reingold Elementary School, Fitchburg, MA
Antoine Djerbaka, Grade 3, Crocker Elementary School, Fitchburg, MA
Cathy Economou, Grade 3, Crocker Elementary School, Fitchburg, MA
Mirriah Elliott, Grade 5, Steck Elementary School, Denver, CO
Julia Fritch, Grade 3, Park Hill Elementary School, Denver, CO
Elizabeth Galindo-Todesco, Grade 4, Doull Elementary School, Denver, CO
Jane Harmon, Grade 3, Green Valley Elementary School, Denver, CO
Cheryl Harris, Grade 4, Green Valley Elementary School, Denver, CO
Debbie Heinz, Grade 3, Steck Elementary School, Denver, CO
Stephanie Henderson, Grade 4, Park Hill Elementary School, Denver, CO
Arlene E. Howard, Fitchburg Public Schools, Fitchburg, MA
Lance Johnson, Grade 5, Memorial Intermediate, Fitchburg, MA
Kyle Kimmal, Grade 3, Green Valley Elementary School, Denver, CO
Maureen Lampa, Grade 3, Reingold Elementary School, Fitchburg, MA
Jennifer Levine, Grade 3, Bay Park Elementary School, San Diego, CA
Pam Magill, Grade 3, Steck Elementary School, Denver, CO

ISBN 13: 978-0-7575-1118-9
ISBN 10: 0-7575-1118-X

10 9 8 7 6 5 4 3 2   10 09 08 07 06

Elizabeth Maki, Grade 3, South Street Elementary School, Fitchburg, MA

Jeannette Martinez, Grade 4, South Street Elementary School, Fitchburg, MA

Lauren McKittrick, Grade 3, Green Valley Elementary School, Denver, CO

Samantha Messier, Denver Public Schools, Denver, CO

Serri Mills, Grade 5, Park Hill Elementary School, Denver, CO

Andrea Oulette, Grade 4, Crocker Elementary School, Fitchburg, MA

Tammi Parisi, Grade 4, Reingold Elementary School, Fitchburg, MA

Carole Pierce, Grade 4, Doull Elementary School, Denver, CO

Marisa Ramirez, San Diego City Schools, San Diego, CA

Soledad Ramirez-Heiler, Grade 4, Wexford Elementary School, Lansing, MI

Christy Ranbarger, Grade 3, Bay Park Elementary School, San Diego, CA

Joan Romano, Grade 4, Reingold Elementary School, Fitchburg, MA

Marci Roy, Grade 3, Reingold Elementary School, Fitchburg, MA

Sabra Scheel, Grade 4, Maple Grove Elementary School, Lansing, MI

Jason Shiroff, Grade 4, Southmoor Elementary School, Denver, CO

Jim Short, Denver Public Schools, Denver, CO

R. Timothy Smith, Lansing School District, Lansing, MI

Catie Solan, Grade 3, Reingold Elementary School, Fitchburg, MA

Hilary Spark, Grade 5, Memorial Intermediate, Fitchburg, MA

Leslie Stahl, Grade 3, Southmoor Elementary School, Denver, CO

Esther Supinski, Grade 3, Crocker Elementary School, Fitchburg, MA

Glenda Swazo, Grade 4, Green Valley Elementary School, Denver, CO

Carrie Symons, Grade 4, Harrington Elementary School, Denver, CO

Randy Jo Thomas, Grade 3, Southmoor Elementary School, Denver, CO

Maria C. Torres, Grade 3, Reingold Elementary School, Fitchburg, MA

Kimberly Toupin, Grade 3, Crocker Elementary School, Fitchburg, MA

Bonnie Walters, Denver Public Schools, Denver, CO

Deborah Welch, Grade 3, Reingold Elementary School, Fitchburg, MA

Connie Wilson, Grade 4, Forest View Elementary School, Lansing, MI

Cindy Wironen, Grade 3, Reingold Elementary School, Fitchburg, MA

Reviewers

Linda Block-Gandy, Mary McMillan Magee, Harold Pratt, Norby Pratt, and Julie L. Norris

Ward's Natural Science, Safety Review

BSCS Staff, First Edition

BSCS Development Team

Nancy M. Landes, Project Director and Author, 1996–1998

Gail C. Foster, Author

Colleen K. Steurer, Author

Vonna G. Pinney, Executive Assistant

Linda K. Ward, Senior Executive Assistant

Rodger W. Bybee, Principal Investigator, 1994–1995

Harold Pratt, Project Director, 1994–1996

Janet Chatlain Girard, Art Coordinator, 1994–1996

BSCS Administrative Staff

Timothy H. Goldsmith, Chair, Board of Directors

Joseph D. McInerney, Director

Michael J. Dougherty, Assistant Director

Lynda B. Micikas, Assistant Director

Larry Satkowiak, Chief Financial Officer

Contributors and Consultants

Randall K. Backe, BSCS, Colorado Springs, Colorado, Contributing Author

Judy L. Capra, Wheat Ridge, Colorado, Freelance Writer

Michael J. Dougherty, BSCS, Colorado Springs, Colorado

B. Ellen Friedman, San Diego, California

Cathy Griswold, Lyons, Oregon, Contributing Author

Jay Hackett, Greeley, Colorado

Debra A. Hannigan, Colorado Springs, Colorado, Contributing Author

David A. Hanych, BSCS, Colorado Springs, Colorado

Karen Hollweg, Washington, DC

Winston King, Bridgetown, Barbados
Paul Kuerbis, Colorado Springs, Colorado
Donald E. Maxwell, BSCS, Colorado Springs, Colorado
Brenda S. McCreight, Colorado Springs, Colorado, Freelance Writer
Mary McMillan, Boulder, Colorado
Marge Melle, Littleton, Colorado, Freelance Writer
Lynda B. Micikas, BSCS, Colorado Springs, Colorado
Jean P. Milani, BSCS, Colorado Springs, Colorado
Renee Mitchell, Lakewood, Colorado, Freelance Writer
Janet Carlson Powell, Boulder, Colorado, Contributing Author
Carol D. Prekker, Broomfield, Colorado, Freelance Writer
Patricia J. Smith, Tucson, Arizona, Freelance Writer
Terry G. Spencer, Monterey, California, Contributing Author
Patti M. Thorn, Austin, Texas, Contributing Author
Bonnie Turnbull, Monument, Colorado, Freelance Writer
Terri B. Weber, Colorado Springs, Colorado
Carol A. Nelson Woller, Boulder, Colorado, Freelance Writer

Field-Test Teachers and Coordinators

Joanne Allen, Westport Elementary School, Westport, Maine
Helene Auger, Westport School District, Westport, Maine
Sheila Dallas, Bethany School, Cincinnati, Ohio
Pat Dobosenski, Pembroke Elementary School, Troy, Michigan
Nina Finkel, Whitter Elementary School, Chicago, Illinois
Mary Elizabeth France, Westport Elementary School, Westport, Maine
Carolyn Gardner, Calhan Elementary School, Calhan, Colorado
Shelly Gordon, Bingham Farms Elementary School, Birmingham, Michigan
Darlene Grunert, Birmingham Public Schools, Birmingham, Michigan
Terry Heinecke, Edgerton Elementary School, Kalispell, Montana
Katherine Hickey, Irving Primary School, Highland Park, New Jersey

Jan Himmelspach, Grayson Elementary School, Waterford, Michigan
Elizabeth Lankes, Bethany School, Glendale, Ohio
Barbara O'Neal, Calhan Elementary School, Calhan, Colorado
Cheryl Pez, Bethany School, Cincinnati, Ohio
Rochelle Rubin, Waterford School District-IMC, Waterford, Michigan
Elizabeth A. Smith, Grayson Elementary School, Waterford, Michigan
Melanie W. Smith, Washington Elementary School, Raleigh, North Carolina
Janet Smith-James, Bartle School, Highland Park, New Jersey
Catherine Snyder, Highland Park School District, Highland Park, New Jersey
Ingrid Snyder, Waterford Village School, Waterford, Michigan
Lee Ann Van Horn, Wake County Public School System, Raleigh, North Carolina
Kathy Wright, Calhan Elementary School, Calhan, Colorado

Reviewers

Marsha Barber, Jefferson County Public Schools, Golden, Colorado
James P. Barufaldi, University of Texas at Austin
Diane Brunner, U.S. Olympic Training Center, Colorado Springs, Colorado
Judy Capra, Jefferson County Public Schools, Golden, Colorado
Candance L. Cline, Etiwanda Elementary School, Etiwanda, California
Larry W. Esposito, University of Colorado at Boulder
Brenda S. Evans, Department of Education, Raleigh, North Carolina
Eva Filsinger, Air Academy High School, Colorado Springs, Colorado
Randy Gray, National Weather Service, Pueblo, Colorado
Leslie Hartten, University of Colorado at Boulder
Steven Holman, Salem, Oregon
Andrew Hudak, University of Colorado at Boulder
Judith Johnson, University of Central Florida, Orlando, Florida
Eric Leonard, The Colorado College, Colorado Springs, Colorado
Ted Lindeman, The Colorado College, Colorado Springs, Colorado

Brownie Linder, Northern Arizona University, Flagstaff, Arizona

Jerry Ludwig, Fox Lane High School, Bedford, New York

Michael J. Madsen, KKTV, Channel 11, Colorado Springs, Colorado

Robert T. Moline, Gustavus Adolphus College, St. Peter, Minnesota

Cherilynn A. Morrow, Space Science Institute, Boulder, Colorado

Rajul Pandya, National Center for Atmospheric Research, Boulder, Colorado

Joseph Pettit, University of Colorado at Boulder

Robert I. Pinney, Colorado Springs, Colorado

Kathleen Roth, Michigan State University, East Lansing, Michigan

Barbara W. Saigo, Saiwood Biology Resources, Montgomery, Alabama

Mary Santlemann, Oregon State University, Corvallis, Oregon

Gail Shroyer, Kansas State University, Manhattan, Kansas

David L. Smith, LaSalle University, Philadelphia, Pennsylvania

Carol Snell, University of Central Florida, Orlando, Florida

John Staver, Kansas State University, Manhattan, Kansas

Joseph Stepans, University of Wyoming, Laramie, Wyoming

Robert Steurer, U.S. West Communications, Colorado Springs, Colorado

Richard Storey, The Colorado College, Colorado Springs, Colorado

Joan Tephly, Marycrest University, Iowa City, Iowa

Lee Vierling, University of Colorado at Boulder

Jack Wheatley, North Carolina State University, Raleigh, North Carolina

Emmet Wright, Kansas State University, Manhattan, Kansas

 Contents

Investigating Ecosystems

Introduction

Doing Science

What is science? What is doing science? What do people do when they do science?

Talk about the following questions with your teammates. Then write your own response to each question in your notebook. Be prepared to discuss your ideas with the class.

1. What is science?

2. What is doing science?

3. What do people do when they do science?

4. What is a scientist like?

5. Can you be a scientist right now?

How Do You Do Science?

Have you ever wondered about anything? Have you ever asked questions about plants, animals, or things? Have you ever investigated to find the answers to your questions? If so, you were doing science! People who do science try to find answers to questions.

As people do science, they wonder and ask questions. They investigate to find answers to their questions. They use their senses and tools to collect information. They keep records as they collect information. They develop explanations to their questions based on information that they have collected. They share ideas and explanations with other people. Sometimes this process leads them to new questions, and the whole process begins again.

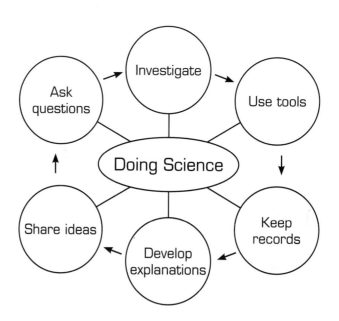

Doing Science Graphic Organizer

During this module, you will do science. You will investigate ecosystems and how living and nonliving things interact.

Ask Questions

Doing science starts with asking a question. People who do science wonder about the world around them. They are curious about objects, animals, plants, or things that happen in the world. What do you think scientists wonder about? What kinds of questions do you think they ask? What do you wonder about? What questions do you ask?

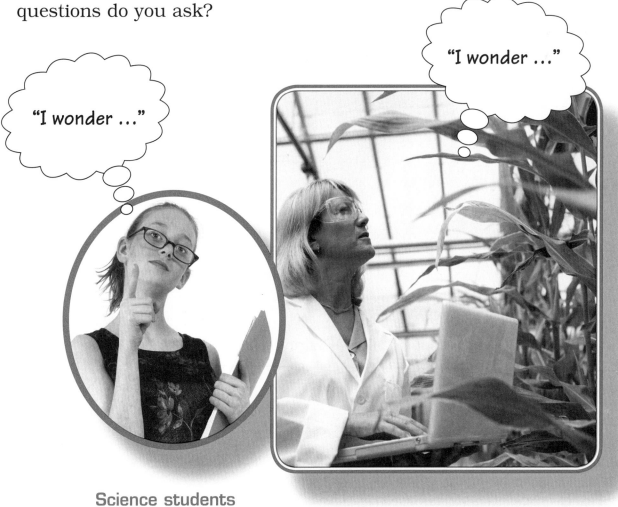

Science students ask questions.

Scientists ask questions.

Investigate

People who do science investigate to find answers to their questions. Sometimes they use their senses to observe things. They describe and compare the objects, materials, and living things that they are investigating. Sometimes they do something to the objects and find out what happens to them. Sometimes they do a fair test and observe what happens. What do you think the scientist in the following photograph might be investigating? What do you think you might be investigating during this module?

Scientists investigate.

Science students investigate.

Use Tools

People who do science use tools, such as thermometers, magnifying glasses, microscopes, and rulers. They use science tools to help them get information, or data, that they cannot get by using just their senses. What tool is the scientist in the following photograph using? What science tools have you used? What kinds of tools do you think you will use during this module?

Scientists use tools.

Science students use tools.

Keep Records

People who do science document data during their investigations. They write, draw, and make charts and graphs. Scientists' documents are called records. Scientists compare their records with the records of other scientists. During this module, you will keep records of your investigations. How might you keep records of your investigations? You will also compare your records with the records of other students.

Science students keep records.

Scientists keep records.

Develop Explanations

One of the important jobs of people who do science is to explain how and why things happen in the world around us. People who do science explain the answers to their questions. They use the data that they have collected to develop explanations. Scientists use their records and data to develop explanations. You will use your records and data to help you explain things.

Science students develop explanations.

Scientists develop explanations.

Share Ideas

People who do science share and discuss their ideas with other people. Sometimes they do their investigations again to find out if the same thing happens another time. Sometimes other people do the same investigation. Then they compare what happened in all the investigations. Scientists share their ideas and explanations. You will share your ideas and explanations with your classmates.

Scientists share their ideas.

Science students share their ideas.

Ask New Questions

One good question leads to another. People who do science are full of questions. As scientists do investigations, they usually think of new questions that they want to answer. Then they do more investigations. Scientists never stop wondering and asking questions about why things are the way they are. We hope that your investigations during this module make you wonder and ask new questions.

Scientists ask new questions.

Science students ask new questions.

Look back at the graphic organizer on page 2 and review the process for doing science. Does the process make sense? Do you think that it is a good way to think about doing science?

Working Together to Do Science

Scientists, engineers, and other people who do science often work in teams so that they can share ideas and tasks. When you do science, you will work in teams too. Sometimes you will work with your friends. Other times, you will work with teammates you don't know as well. You may stay in the same team through several lessons. Teammates have responsibilities as they work together.

All teammates are responsible for

- doing the task well and

- helping their teammates understand the task and what the team did.

Team Skills

It is easier to do your team task well if you practice some team skills while you work. You will use the following five team skills every time you work in a team.

Team Skills

1. Move into your team quickly and quietly.
2. Stay with your team.
3. Speak softly.
4. Share and take turns.
5. Do your job.

1. **Move into your team quickly and quietly.** When your teacher tells you to meet with your team, find your teammates right away. Go directly to your team's meeting place without stopping to talk along the way.

2. **Stay with your team.** This skill means that you pay attention to your teammates and work with them to do your task. You do not wander around the room and talk to other teams.

3. **Speak softly.** When you talk with your teammates, keep your voice down so only your teammates can hear you.

4. **Share and take turns.** The skill of sharing and taking turns takes some practice. You and your teammates must make sure that everyone on the team gets to do part of each investigation and to share his or her ideas.

5. **Do your job.** When you work as a team, each teammate will be responsible for one job that helps the team (materials manager, tracker, messenger, or skill builder). You might like one job more than the others, but each job is important for the team. You will have a chance to do all the jobs at some time. The job descriptions are on pages 14–15. Whenever your teammates change jobs, review the descriptions so that everyone will remember what to do.

Sometimes your team will practice special skills that will help you work better together. Read the special skills and talk about them with your teacher. Describe what your team will say and do to practice each special skill.

■ *Special Team Skills*

1. Listen when others talk.

2. Discuss many ideas before selecting one.

3. Criticize ideas, not people.

1. Listen when others talk. How can you show that you are really listening to a teammate? How can you make sure that every teammate has a chance to talk?

2. Discuss many ideas before selecting one. Do you know the old saying "Two heads are better than one"? If you put three heads together in a team, just think of how many ideas you can have! This skill will help you remember to let each teammate share ideas before the team decides on one answer or way to do something.

3. **Criticize ideas, not people.** Has anyone ever made fun of you or said something unkind because of something you said? When that happened, how did you feel about yourself and about the other person? Sometimes people have different opinions or ideas, or they want to do things differently. That is the beauty of teamwork. You can share many ideas and learn something in a way you never could have thought of by yourself. If you don't agree with a teammate's idea, you can say you disagree and then give your idea. You can say, "That's one idea. Here is another idea."

Sometimes when people disagree, they say unkind things about the person who said the idea, like, "Do you really think that? You must be pretty stupid." When you disagree with a teammate, tell him or her what you disagree with rather than calling your teammate names. Disagreeing with ideas is helpful for your team because it will make you think through your ideas more clearly. You will probably feel more like offering your own ideas if you know that others won't call you names or put you down.

These job descriptions will help you remember what to do when it is your turn to do each job. There is a special colored wristband to wear for each job.

The **materials manager** gets the supplies that are listed under the heading "Team Supplies." When the team finishes the team task, everyone helps clean up the work area. Then the materials manager returns the supplies to the supply table.

The **tracker** keeps track of what the team is doing. The tracker makes sure that the team does every step and follows the directions in order. The tracker might point to each step as the team works on it. If the team needs to stop, the tracker might write the number of the step where the team stopped. Everyone on the team needs to help read and follow the directions. The tracker is not the team's only reader.

If the team gets stuck, the **messenger** may ask another team's messenger for help. Or the messenger may ask your teacher for help. Only the messenger can leave the team and ask for help, though. Everyone else should stay with the team.

The **skill builder** encourages teammates to practice the team skills. The skill builder tells teammates when they are doing the skill well and reminds teammates to listen to one another and to be polite and courteous. The skill builder helps teammates work together and complete the team task.

Doing Science with C.Q. and I.O.

Hi, I'm C.Q.

C.Q. and I.O. are characters in your student guide. C.Q. is curious and asks a lot of questions. That is how he got his name. I.O. got her name because she likes to investigate things and observe carefully.

C.Q. and I.O. like to work together to find answers to their questions. Sometimes they will give you some questions to investigate or some problems to solve. They invite you to become curious and questioning too. Look for C.Q. and I.O. for helpful hints and reminders!

Hi, I'm I.O.

Making and Using a Science Notebook

Scientists document what they do by writing, drawing, and making charts and graphs. They call what they write or draw a record. When you do science, you need to keep records of what you do too. Most of the time, you will keep your records in a science notebook.

A science notebook is like a diary. In it, you keep all your records about what happens in an investigation. What you write in a notebook also helps you remember what you did, how you did it, what you observed, when something happened, and what you learned. The icon of the notebook will help you remember when to record something, but you can use your notebook at other times too.

Each time you check on an investigation, you should record your data in your notebook. You can draw pictures, take measurements, and write descriptions of what you observed or how you did something. You can add special pages like calendar pages or handouts to your notebook. The more information you record in your notebook, the easier it will be to describe what happened during your investigation. Your records will also help you explain why you think something happened.

In your notebook, you can keep track of questions you wonder about. Then you can design your own investigations to find the answers to your questions.

Doing Science Safely

Doing science is interesting and a lot of fun. But just like scientists, you might sometimes work with equipment and materials that could cause harm to you or your clothing. When you see the caution hand, pay special attention to the safety hints. Remember to always handle your materials and equipment exactly as the directions say you should. Even common, everyday items can be hazardous when not handled carefully!

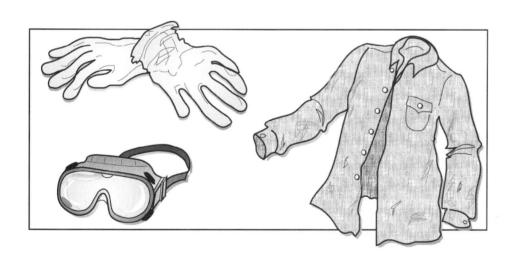

Previewing the Student Guide

Take a tour of your guide with your teacher.

1. Locate the table of contents. How is a table of contents helpful?

2. Locate the glossary. How is a glossary helpful?

3. Select a lesson.

   a. Look through the lesson looking for titles, headings, and subheadings. What clues do the text sizes give you about the lesson?

   b. Locate the "Team Task," "Team Skills," "Team Jobs," "Team Supplies," and "Directions" sections. How are these things organized to help you learn?

   c. Look for visual clues (photographs, illustrations, charts, graphs, and icons). How can these clues help you learn?

   d. Look for boldfaced words. Why would some words be boldfaced?

4. Look through another lesson. How are the lessons similar? How are they different?

5. How can this guide help you learn? How can it help you think like a scientist?

Digging In!

You have learned a little about doing science. You have begun to think about what it means to do science. You have reviewed the importance of working as a team. You have talked about team skills and special team skills. You have looked at team job descriptions. You know that C.Q. and I.O. are eager helpers. You have made your science notebook. You know what sign to look for to make sure that you work safely. You have also previewed the text to understand how it is organized to help you learn. Now it is time to put on your scientist cap and begin doing science!

Lesson 1

Imagine Yourself

Where do you live? In the city? In the country? How would you describe the environment where you live? What is the weather like? What is the land like? What plants, animals, and nonliving things can be found where you live?

The environment where you live has its own character that makes it different from other places. If someone asked you to describe the area where you live, you probably could tell him or her a lot!

Peeped in a pond?
Relaxed in a reef?
Moved on a mountain?

Crawled on the coast?
Swam in a swamp?
Frolicked in a forest?

But what if you had to move to another place—a different, unfamiliar place? What if you weren't you? What if you . . .

Describe the place you imagined. Name other things you might find there. Tell about what happens in the new place where you live.

Deepen Understanding through Vocabulary

1. Complete a "4-Square Chart" for the term interact.

2. Be prepared to share your chart with the class.

Video Adventure

Without leaving the classroom, you and your classmates can travel to different places. But you can't go unless you have a ticket! Where is your special destination?

Team Task

Choose team tickets to travel. Watch the video and list the living and nonliving things that are found in the places to which your team travels. Describe the environment and what happens in each place.

Team Jobs

Tracker

Messenger

Skill Builder

Team Skills

Move into your team quickly and quietly.

Stay with your team.

Speak softly.

Share and take turns.

Team Supplies

- 3 travel tickets
- 1 ruler
- each teammate's notebook

- 3 pencils
- 3 wristbands
- 1 plastic tray

1. Choose three travel tickets.

    a. Each teammate should choose one ticket.

    b. Make sure that you each have a ticket to a different place.

2. Look at each teammate's ticket.

    a. In your notebook, describe what you think each place is like.

    b. Name some animals and plants that you think live in each place.

3. After talking with your team, write in your notebook the best ideas about the place printed on your travel ticket.

    a. Write "My Best Ideas" at the top of the list or choose another title for your list.

    b. Describe what you think the place is like.

    c. Describe the animals you might find there.

    d. Describe the plants you might find there.

4. Make a data table like the following one to record your observations from the video.

Living Things	Nonliving Things	Interactions

Use the ruler to make straight lines. Leave enough space to write your observations.

5. Go on the video adventure.

Carefully observe your teammates' travel places too.

a. Watch for your travel place. Then observe carefully!

b. List living things you observe in the first column of your data table.

c. List nonliving things you observe in the second column of your data table.

d. List interactions that you observe in the last column of your data table.

6. On a new page in your notebook, describe your travel place.

    a. Is this a dry place or a watery place?

    b. Is this a warm or a cold place?

7. Compare your description with what you listed under "My Best Ideas."

    a. Which of your best ideas did you observe in the video?

    b. Do you have to change some of your ideas?

✓ Checking Understanding

Part A: Talk about the following questions with your teammates. Then write or draw your own response to each question in your notebook. Be prepared to share your responses with the class.

1. What is the same about all three travel places?

2. What is different about the three travel places?

3. In which place would you rather live? Why would you rather live there?

Part B: Review the "Doing Science" section on pages 1–19. Look at the graphic organizer on page 2. Talk about ways that you were doing science during this lesson. Then, on your own, describe ways in which you were doing science in your notebook.

Part C: Think about the activities that you did and the strategies that you used during this lesson. Talk about the following questions with your teammates. Then write your own response to each question in your notebook.

1. What did you learn during this lesson?

2. What activities or strategies helped you learn? How or why were they helpful?

3. Did working as a team help you learn? Why or why not?

4. What skills did your team do well? What skills does your team need to improve?

Lesson 2

Study Systems

In the last lesson, you caught a glimpse of living and nonliving things that are found in different places. You also saw how some living and nonliving things interact with one another. What interactions do you think happen where you live?

Exploring What Happens Out-of-Doors

The world has many kinds of places to explore—forests, grasslands, deserts, oceans, and mountains. Visiting faraway places is exciting! It is especially exciting for scientists who

explore what happens in nature. Scientists, such as botanists, ecologists, and wildlife biologists, "do science" in natural areas. They do the things you read about in the "Doing Science" lesson.

Scientists find out what happens in nature by asking questions, observing, and uncovering clues that lead to new questions. Scientists begin by asking questions such as the following:

- What is the landscape like?

- What is the weather like?

- What kinds of nonliving things are in this place?

- What kinds of plants and animals live in this place?

- What kind of "homes" do the animals make?

- What do the animals eat?

- How do the plants meet their needs to survive?

- How do the plants and animals interact?

During their investigations, scientists make observations to find answers to their questions. By observing, recording their observations, making sense of their observations, and sharing their data with other scientists, they learn more about how plants and animals interact with their environment and with one another.

You can do these things too! You can explore what goes on in nature by asking questions, making observations, and uncovering clues.

Exploring Your Own Study Systems

Throughout this module, you will be exploring and observing two systems. One will be inside. You will set up and observe an indoor pond. The other will be outside. Your outside system will probably be somewhere on your school grounds.

Team Task

As you explore your study systems, you will make daily observations, keep records in your science notebook, and ask questions about the systems. You will share your observations and records with your classmates.

Team Jobs

Materials Manager

Tracker

Messenger

Team Skills

Listen when others talk.

Team Supplies

- 3 hand lenses
- each teammate's notebook
- crayons or markers
- 3 pencils
- 3 wristbands

Directions for Observing Your Study Systems

1. Visit each study system as often as possible.

2. Keep detailed records in your notebook.

   a. Draw pictures and write about what you observe.

   b. Draw pictures and write about any changes you observe.

Write the date on each picture or notebook entry.

Be patient! Not all changes happen overnight.

3. Ask questions and look for clues to answer the questions. Your questions might be something like these:

a. How many different kinds of plants and animals are in each study system?

b. What do the animals eat?

c. Where do the animals live?

d. When are the animals active and when are they quiet?

e. What size are the plants?

f. Do the plants stay the same size?

g. What changes do you notice from day to day?

h. Can you find clues that animals live in the study system, even if you can't see them? **Hint:** Has something chewed on tree bark or leaves? Do you see droppings on the ground? Do you see feathers, hair, or tracks?

i. What is the weather like outdoors?

j. What is the temperature?

k. What is the landscape like outdoors?

Using Your Science Notebook

Throughout this module, you will record observations in your notebook. Think of your notebook as a daily log. It will help you remember what you observed in the study systems. You decide how to organize your notebook and what to write in it.

You can set up a notebook by writing the date, time, place, and weather conditions. You can include detailed drawings of your observations of plants and animals. You can write notes about what you did, what you observed, what questions you had, and ideas you had.

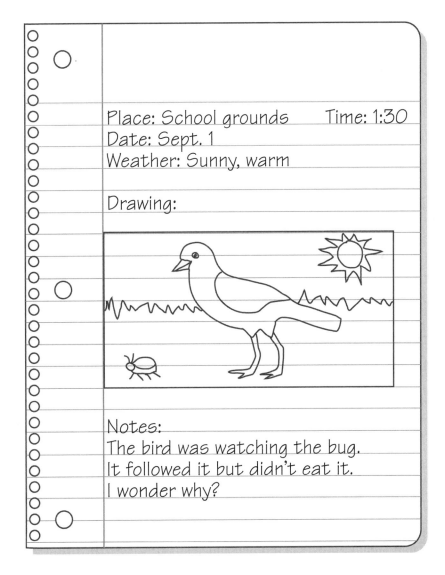

Place: School grounds   Time: 1:30
Date: Sept. 1
Weather: Sunny, warm

Drawing:

Notes:
The bird was watching the bug.
It followed it but didn't eat it.
I wonder why?

Interaction Data Table				
Date	Place	Living or Nonliving Thing	Interaction or Change	My Evidence

You can make an "Interaction data table" to keep track of any interactions you observe between living things and between living and nonliving things. When you have evidence of an interaction, write down the date, the names of the things that interacted, and how they interacted. On separate pages, you can write about or draw the details of the changes to show how the study systems look as they change.

You might take photographs of the system. You can put the photographs in your notebook to show how the system has changed or stayed the same.

Bird Observations

May 1

10:00 am-10:15 am

We saw 10 Chickadees taking turns at the feeder. 8 Juncos were on the ground eating seed that dropped from the feeder.

May 2

10:00 am-10:15 am

Today Evening Grosbeaks joined the Chickadees at the feeder.

6 Grosbeaks (3 male, 3 female)

10 Chickadees

8 Juncos eating from the ground again.

Here's a list of ideas you might want to record in your notebook. Add your own ideas to the list too!

- What does the place look like when you first see it?

- What living things do you see (the kinds, numbers, and descriptions)?

- What nonliving things do you see (the kinds, numbers, and descriptions)?

- How do the living things change (size, color, shape, numbers) during your observations?

- How do the nonliving things change (color, shape, location, amount) during your observations?

- How do the living and nonliving things interact?

- Has anything interesting happened?

The more information you record in your notebook, the easier it will be to remember interactions and to find out how nature works in the study systems. Be sure to write down any questions you have about the things or interactions in your study systems. If you have ideas for finding answers to the questions, write the ideas down too. As you explore the study systems, you will uncover clues and find answers to the questions!

Sharing Ideas

No matter what kind of a study system you explore, you will need to make careful observations to uncover clues and discover patterns in how nature works. How does someone make careful observations?

Can you think of other tips for observing a study system?

Tips for Observing a Study System

1. **Walk slowly and step lightly.** In an outdoor setting, if you let branches crack underfoot, the sound may frighten animals away. Moving slowly lets you observe things that others miss.

2. **Wait patiently and keep your eyes and ears open.** Do you know how to look up and down as well as straight ahead? Can you find animal tracks? Can you spot an animal that is holding perfectly still? Can you find evidence of an interaction, like a chewed leaf or a rock that has been moved? Do you know how to pretend that your eyes are a camera and make a picture of a place in your head?

3. **Observe with your nose.** What kinds of smells do you notice? Are they pleasant or are they bad? Can you smell a pile of pine needles or a rotting log before your eyes spot it?

continued on next page

4. **Keep quiet.** Talking, especially loud talking or whistling, will scare away most of the birds and animals you hope to see. Being quiet in an outdoor place lets you hear sounds such as birds calling and squirrels chattering. Being quiet around a classroom study system lets you hear sounds of movement.

How Could You Find Out?

Design an investigation to find out the answers to these questions, or write questions that interest you.

- What kind of food do the animals in your study systems prefer?

- Do some animals eat only some parts of food?

- Does an animal in your study systems have special body parts that help it get food?

- How many different kinds of food does one animal eat?

- How do animals interact over a piece of food?

- How do two different kinds of animals that eat the same food interact?

- Can an animal find its food if the food is hidden under something?

- Do different sizes of the same food attract different animals?

- Does the same food in different places attract different animals?

- How much food does an animal eat in a day?

- Do different kinds of plants have different kinds of insects feeding on them?

- Which insects make which kinds of marks on leaves?

- Do some insects eat the insects that are eating plants?

- On which parts of plants do camouflaged insects feed?

- How fast do the plants in this system grow?

- Do the plants in the system produce flowers, seeds, or fruit?

Lesson 3

Nature's Cafeteria

How do Kweet, bees, Wogs, Beezlenut Trees, and trout interact? Read the following passage from *Scrambled Eggs Super!* by Dr. Seuss. In your notebook, draw a picture that shows your ideas about the interactions.

I went for the kind that were mellow and sweet
And the world's sweetest eggs are the eggs of the Kweet
Which is due to those very sweet trout which they eat
And those trout . . . well, they're sweet 'cause they only
    eat Wogs
And Wogs, after all, are the world's sweetest frogs
And the reason they're sweet is whenever they lunch
It's always the world's sweetest bees that they munch
And the reason no bees can be sweeter than these . . .
They only eat blossoms off Beezlenut Trees
And these Beezlenut Blossoms are sweeter than sweet
And that's why I nabbed several eggs from the Kweet.

Share your drawings of the interactions from *Scrambled Eggs Super.*

1. How are the drawings alike and different?

2. What do all the drawings show?

3. Do these kinds of interactions happen in every environment? Why do you think so?

Food, Glorious Food

The passage from *Scrambled Eggs Super!* is all about meeting one basic need of living things— the need for food! What is food? Why do animals need food?

Animals, including humans, eat food for energy and nutrients. Food energy is necessary for all animals to grow, move, reproduce, and stay alive. All living things must find, catch, or make the food they need. Different kinds of living things need different kinds of food. Many kinds of animals and plants are connected through the food they eat, just like the Kweets, trout, Wogs, bees, and Beezlenut Trees. Find out about food connections by investigating a "meadow cafeteria."

Investigating a Meadow Cafeteria

When one animal eats another animal or a plant, it becomes part of a chain—a food chain. Food chains show what munches on what—who lunches on whom. Food chains also show the order of what gets eaten by what. As you play the Food Chain Game, think about the reason for the food chain. What gets passed along the chain from one living thing to another?

■ *Team Task*

Link all the possible food chain game cards to make food chains that you might find in a meadow. Draw your completed food chains in your notebook.

■ *Team Jobs*

Tracker

Messenger

Skill Builder

■ *Team Skills*

Listen when others talk

■ Team Supplies

- 1 pair of scissors

- 1 copy of "Food Chain Game Cards"

- 2 copies of "Arrow Cards"

- 1 envelope

- 1 sheet of chart paper

- each teammate's notebook

- markers or crayons

- 3 pencils

- 3 wristbands

- 1 plastic tray

Directions

1. Cut apart the food chain game cards and separate the food chain game cards from the arrow cards.

2. Spread out the food chain game cards so that you can see all of them easily.

3. Using two food chain game cards and one arrow card, make a food connection that you might find in a meadow.

    a. Talk about how to arrange the food chain game cards and arrow cards.

    b. Read the food connection and decide if it makes sense.

4. Look at the following example of a food connection.

    a. Compare it with the food connection you made.

    b. Decide if you need to change your food connection from step 3.

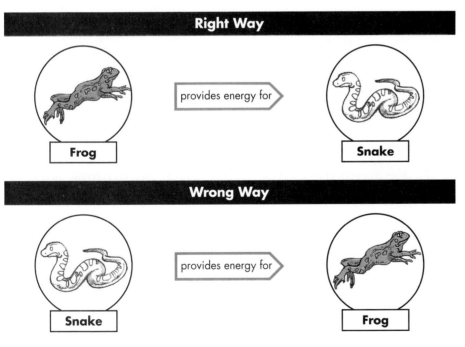

A snake eats a frog, but
a frog does not eat a snake . . .

Be sure to read your food chain each time you make a connection. Do you all agree that the arrow points the right way?

You can write or draw your food chains in your notebook.

5. Connect as many round game cards and arrow cards as you can to make meadow food chains.

   a. Try to make chains with more than one connection.

   b. What is the longest chain you can make?

6. Record your food chains in your notebook.

7. Read "Energy and Food Chains" on pages 49–53.

8. Look at your food chains again.

   a. Make changes to the food chains if the team agrees.

   b. In your notebook, show the changes you made in your food chains.

9. Draw at least four of your food chains on your chart paper.

10. Be prepared to share your food chains with the class.

Energy and Food Chains

Where do you get the energy to work and play? Your body needs energy to grow, move, and stay alive. You get the energy that you need from the foods that you eat.

Other animals need energy too. Animals get the energy they need from the foods that they eat. Some animals eat just plants. Some animals eat plants and other animals. Some animals eat just other animals.

What about plants? Do they need energy? Plants need energy to grow and stay alive too. Plants don't eat so where do they get the energy they need?

Using the food chains you recorded in your notebook, talk about the answers to these questions with your classmates.

1. Where are plants located in food chains? Where are animals located in food chains?

2. Where did you place the Sun card in the food chains?

3. How are some food chains different?

4. How are all food chains the same?

5. Do some plants and animals in food chains have more than one arrow next to them? Explain your answer.

6. Look at what you drew from *Scrambled Eggs Super*. Did you draw a food chain? Explain your answer.

7. What gets passed along the chain from one living thing to another?

Food Chains to Food Webs

Did all your food chains from the game card activity go in a straight line? You might have discovered that food interactions in nature's cafeteria don't always flow in straight lines. Think about a chipmunk, for example. Chipmunks eat different kinds of plant parts, such as acorns and other nuts, berries, bulbs, and seedlings. Chipmunks also eat small animals like grasshoppers, ants, and earthworms.

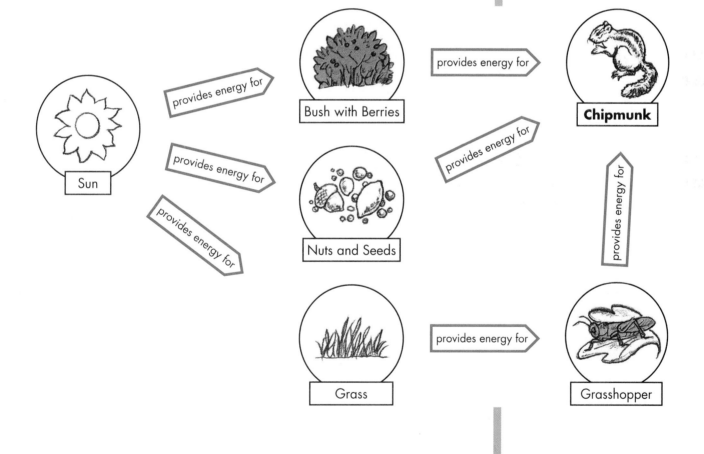

Chipmunks become dinner for many different kinds of animals, including weasels, bobcats, foxes, coyotes, and hawks.

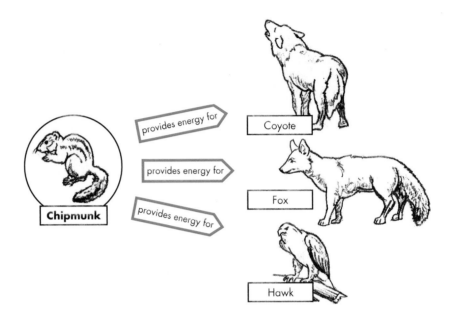

Some of the animals that eat chipmunks eat some of the same things that chipmunks eat too. If all these food connections are drawn on one page, they look like the next illustration.

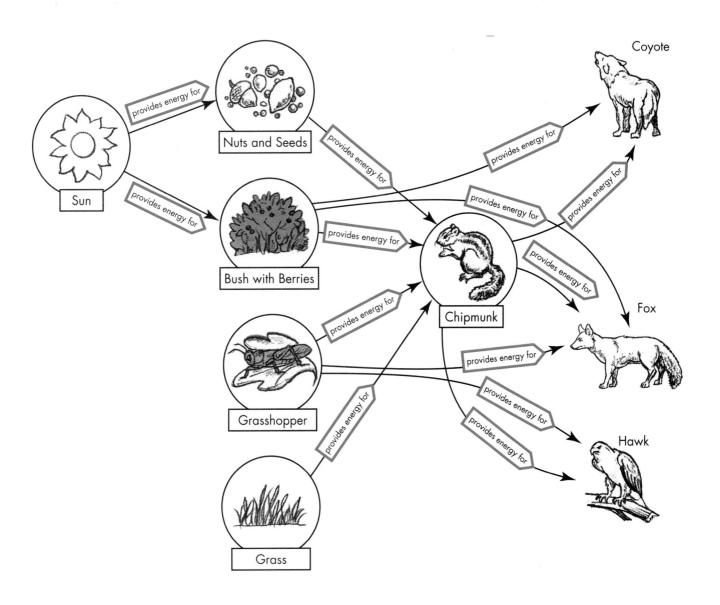

This is an example of a **food web**. Why do you think this is called a food web and not a food chain? Trace the food chains within the web to find all the connections.

Look at the next food web. It shows an ocean food web that you might find near Antarctica. Tiny green plants, called phytoplankton, grow in the water. In the ocean, just like on land, food interactions begin with green plants that get their energy from the Sun. Tiny animals eat the phytoplankton to get energy. Small animals, such as krill, feed on the tiny animals. (Krill are small animals that look like shrimp.) All the small animals and plants are food for bigger animals, such as fish and squid, seals, penguins, and whales.

In the ocean, just like on land, plants and animals are linked through food chains. Because animals eat different kinds of plants and other animals, the food chains become linked together in food webs.

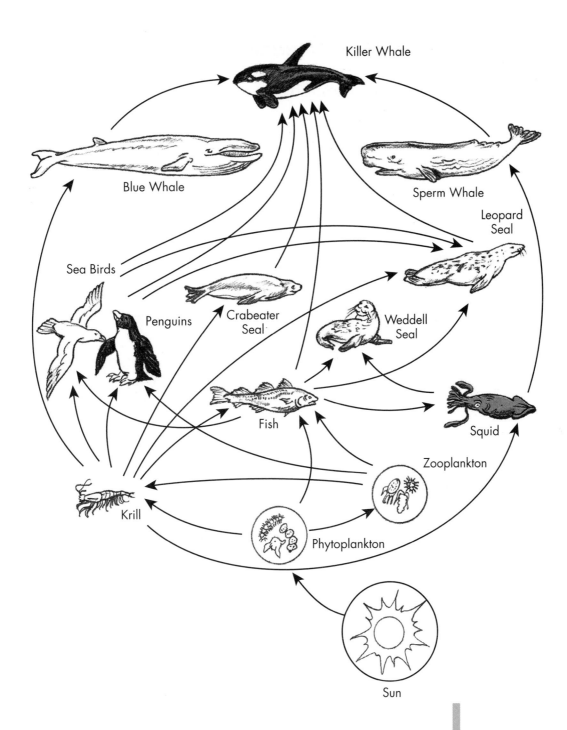

Killer Whale

Blue Whale

Sperm Whale

Leopard Seal

Sea Birds

Penguins

Crabeater Seal

Weddell Seal

Fish

Squid

Zooplankton

Krill

Phytoplankton

Sun

All living things in the food web depend on one another—and ultimately on the energy from the Sun—for their food. What would happen to the ocean food web if the phytoplankton disappeared?

Creating a Meadow Food Web

What do you think a food web might look like in a meadow? Your team will use the food chain game cards to create a meadow food web. This time, you might need to use reference books to help you decide how the food chains connect to make a food web.

■ *Team Task*

Connect the food chain game cards to show a food web in a meadow. Use all of the round game cards. (You may make additional game cards too.) Record the food web in your notebook.

■ *Team Jobs*

Tracker

Messenger

Skill Builder

■ *Team Skills*

Listen when others talk.

Team Supplies

- 1 pair of scissors

- 1 set of food chain game cards and arrow cards

- 5 index cards, 3" × 5"

- each teammate's notebook

- markers or crayons

- 3 pencils

- 3 wristbands

Directions

1. Place the food chain game cards and arrow cards into the food chains you made in the first part of this lesson.

2. Connect the food chains to make a meadow food web.

   a. If you do not agree or are not sure how to connect the food chains, use reference materials to find out what the different animals eat.

   b. Add arrow cards to show all the connections between the food chains.

Use your notebook records to help you.

3. Using the index cards, markers, and scissors, make new round game cards or arrow cards that fit within your food web.

4. Add the new cards to your food web.

5. Record your team's food web in your notebook.

6. Be ready to share your food web with the class.

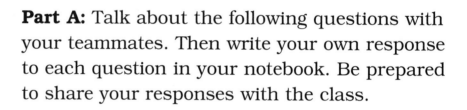

✓ Checking Understanding

Part A: Talk about the following questions with your teammates. Then write your own response to each question in your notebook. Be prepared to share your responses with the class.

1. How is a food web different from a food chain? You may draw examples if you wish.

2. Would you put the Sun card in every food chain or food web? Why or why not?

3. What would happen to the food web if the green plants disappeared from the meadow?

4. Draw a food chain or a food web for the system that your class is observing from lesson 2.

Part B: Review the "Doing Science" section on pages 1–19. Look at the graphic organizer on page 2. Talk about ways that you were doing science during this lesson. Then, on your own, describe ways in which you were doing science in your notebook.

Part C: Think about the activities that you did and the strategies that you used during this lesson. Talk about the following questions with your teammates. Then write your own response to each question in your notebook.

1. What did you learn during this lesson?

2. What activities or strategies helped you learn? How or why were they helpful?

3. Did working as a team help you learn? Why or why not?

4. What skills did your team do well? What skills does your team need to improve?

 **Lesson 4**

Making Connections

So far in this module, you have explored
interactions between living and nonliving things
in different kinds of places—places like oceans,
deserts, ponds, and meadows.

As you have discovered in previous lessons, all of these places have plants, animals, and nonliving things that interact to make the system work. Often the plants and animals in one place are quite different from the plants and animals in another place, but they also are the same in some ways. How can that be?

Food: Making It, Eating It, and Rotting It

As you learned in lesson 3, plants and animals often interact because animals need food! Food interactions are interesting to **ecologists**. Ecologists are scientists who study interactions between living and nonliving things. They study interactions in all kinds of places.

By studying food interactions, ecologists have found that there are similar groups of living things in all places. To make sense of the natural world, ecologists have divided living things into a few groups according to the "job" the living things do in nature.

Those groups are the producers, the consumers, and the decomposers.

Producers

The first group contains all the living things that make or produce food energy. They use energy from the Sun to produce food energy. Because they produce their own food, these living things are called **producers**. In most places, producers are green plants.

There are many kinds of producers. Banana trees, dandelions, pine trees, grasses, rosebushes, algae, and phytoplankton are all producers.

Consumers

Other kinds of living things cannot make their own food. They must hunt, catch, trap, or otherwise get food to provide the energy they need to stay alive. These living things are called **consumers** because they consume other living things. There are many kinds of consumers.

Some consumers eat just plants. Some consumers eat just animals. Some consumers eat both plants and animals. Other consumers "clean up" by eating dead plants and animals. Caterpillars, elephants, snails, starfishes, raccoons, and crabs are consumers. What about you? Are you a consumer too?

Decomposers

Molds, mushrooms, and bacteria make up a special group called **decomposers**. These living things do not produce, catch, or trap food. They get their food energy from dead plants and animals. The job of the decomposers is to break down dead plants and animals and return them to the soil. In this way, the matter that

makes up all living things is "recycled" so that new plants growing in the soil can use the nutrients from the dead plants and animals.

Think about what you just read and the meadow food web you created in lesson 3. Talk about the following questions with your teammates. Then write your own response to each question in your notebook.

1. Which living things were producers?

2. Which living things were consumers?

3. Which living things were decomposers?

More Interactions: Mouse in the Meadow

You just read about the food interactions between living things. Are there other interactions between living and nonliving things that an ecologist might find interesting?

An ecologist studies all the connections between living and nonliving things in the natural world. Let's take what you know about a mouse and look at it from an ecologist's point of view.

How Might an Ecologist Look at a Mouse in an Ecosystem?

Think about a mouse that lives in a meadow. What does the mouse need to survive?

How does a mouse meet its needs for food, water, shelter, and space? Do the mouse's interactions with both living and nonliving things determine how much or how little the mouse grows?

What Does a Mouse Eat?

In lesson 3, you used food chains and food webs to show how a mouse meets its needs for food.

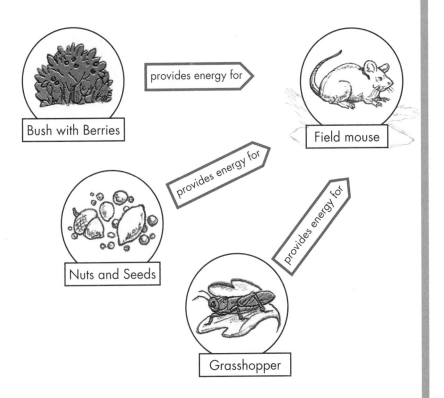

Bush with Berries

provides energy for

Field mouse

provides energy for

Nuts and Seeds

provides energy for

Grasshopper

How Does a Mouse Interact with Nonliving Things in Its Ecosystem?

A mouse drinks water and breathes the air. It builds its nest on the ground under the trees using fallen leaves and bits of fur. The mouse doesn't build its nest out in the open. It hides the nest in tall grass or in a dead tree stump so that predators, like a hawk flying overhead, won't see the nest. What might happen if the hawk spotted the nest of baby mice?

What Would an Ecologist Find Out?

There are all kinds of interactions between the mouse and the environmental resources—other living and nonliving things—that the mouse needs to survive.

You already know the following:

- The mouse interacts with insects, seeds, nuts, and fruit to meet its needs for food.

- The mouse must interact with water and air to survive.

- The mouse interacts with fallen leaves, bits of fur, a dead tree stump, or tall grass in the forest to meet its needs for shelter and space.

- The mouse also might interact with a hawk or another hungry animal, but not in a way that helps the mouse to survive!

An ecologist would also find out the following:

- The mouse interacts with the Sun, both directly and indirectly. The mouse interacts directly with the Sun when the Sun provides warmth and light for the mouse. The mouse uses the Sun's energy indirectly when it eats parts of plants for food or uses parts of plants for building its nest.

- When the mouse dies, the body will be broken down by decomposers like bacteria and fungi. Once the body is broken down, it provides nutrients for the soil.

An ecologist might organize his or her notes about mouse interactions as a graphic organizer.

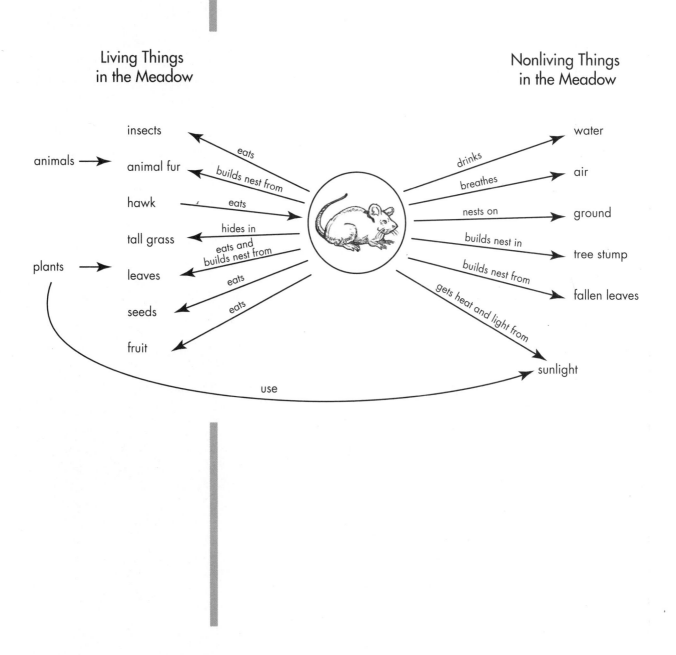

Living Things
in the Meadow

Nonliving Things
in the Meadow

animals →

insects

animal fur — builds nest from

hawk — eats

tall grass — hides in

plants → leaves — eats and builds nest from

seeds — eats

fruit — eats

eats

drinks — water

breathes — air

nests on — ground

builds nest in — tree stump

builds nest from — fallen leaves

gets heat and light from — sunlight

use

You just looked at a mouse like an ecologist. You looked at many of the interactions a mouse might have with living and nonliving things in its meadow environment.

Reflective Pause

Think about an animal with which you are familiar as an ecologist does. Talk about the following questions with your teammates. Then write your own response to each question in your notebook.

1. What is your animal?

2. How does your animal interact with its environment to meet its needs for food, water, shelter, and space?

Team Task

Show the interactions between living and nonliving things in three ecosystems. Share your ideas.

Team Jobs

Materials Manager

Tracker

Messenger

Team Skills

Discuss many ideas before selecting one.

Team Supplies

- 1 copy of "Oak Forest Ecopicture," "Tropical Rain Forest Ecopicture," or "Salt Marsh Ecopicture"

- 2 sheets of chart paper

- each teammate's notebook

- markers or crayons

- 3 pencils

- 3 wristbands

- 1 plastic tray

1. Read about one of the following ecosystems with your teammates: an oak forest, a tropical rain forest, or a salt marsh. (See pages 81–95.)

2. List the living and nonliving things mentioned in the reading.

3. Look at the ecopicture that matches the ecosystem that you read about.

   a. Can you find living and nonliving things that you read about?

   b. Are there additional living and nonliving things in the ecopicture? If so, add them to your list.

4. On your first sheet of chart paper, create a chart like the following one. Classify all the living things in your ecosystem as producers, consumers, or decomposers.

Producers	Consumers	Decomposers

5. Label your second sheet of chart paper "Interactions." Draw or describe interactions for food, water, shelter, or space that you read about or think might happen based on your ecopicture. Make sure that you provide at least one example for each need.

6. Be prepared to share your charts with the class.

An Oak Forest

You can watch the seasons change in an oak forest. In the spring, the oak trees bud and new green leaves appear. The trees' green leaves use the light energy from the Sun to make food energy so that the trees can survive and grow. Melting snow and rainfall provide water for the trees to use. In the summer, the oak trees make hundreds of seeds, called acorns.

Squirrels, small birds, and other animals eat many of the acorns. Some drop onto the soil and begin to grow into new trees. In the fall, the oak leaves change color and fall off the trees. By winter, the branches are bare. The soil under the trees becomes dark and rich during the fall and winter months. This happens because the leaves that fall from the trees return nutrients from the trees to the soil as the decomposers in the soil help the leaves decay.

Many types of plants and animals live and grow in the rich soil beneath the oak trees. If you walk through an oak forest,

you might see mushrooms growing among the decaying leaves and soil. These strange plants don't use the Sun's light as energy to make their own food as green plants do. Instead, they get their energy by breaking down the dead tree leaves.

Some small animals, such as moles, tunnel in the soil and eat plant bulbs, insects, spiders, and earthworms. As earthworms tunnel underground and through leaf litter, they eat seeds, dead plant parts, bits of mushrooms, and parts of dead animals. The tunnels help the plants by allowing air into the soil and creating space for their roots.

Other types of plants and animals also live and grow in the oak forest. Besides oak trees, many types of bushes, grasses, and flowering plants grow in the rich soil. The trees, bushes, grasses, and other plants produce leaves, berries, and seeds that become food for small birds, mice, raccoons, and deer.

Some birds, such as robins, catch earthworms to eat. Owls eat insects, smaller birds, mice, moles, and squirrels. Woodpeckers make holes in tree trunks to get at the insects that are underneath the bark. Frogs eat spiders and insects. Snakes may eat insects, spiders, frogs, mice, other snakes, small birds, bird eggs, and moles. Spiders spin webs between tree branches to catch insects.

The forest also provides many forms of shelter and water sources. Birds build nests in the trees and shrubs. Small animals hide in holes in the trees.

The color of some animals helps them hide in the leaves of the trees or blend in with the bark so predators cannot easily find them. When it rains or when the snow melts, water collects on the forest floor in puddles, ponds, and rivers from which animals can drink.

A Tropical Rain Forest

A tropical rain forest is hot, humid, and filled with plants. Tropical rain forests are found near the equator. They remain green and warm all year long. They receive rainfall almost every day. In fact, walking through a tropical rain forest might remind you of walking through a greenhouse.

The tropical rain forest is home to more than half of all the world's different types of plants and animals. Plants like vines, orchids, ferns, teak, mahogany, bananas, coffee, and rubber grow in tropical rain forests. These plants need plenty of water, sunlight, and warmth to help them grow. The plants produce food for the animals that live in the tropical rain forest.

One plant in the tropical rain forest doesn't need soil or roots to grow. It grows on a tree trunk or branch. Most people call it an air plant because it appears to grow using only the air. The center of the plant looks like a cup. The cup area traps rainwater. The plant absorbs water from the cup area to help it grow. Many small insects, spiders, frogs, and birds get food and water from the plant. Some frogs and insects even lay their eggs in the cup area.

Even though the soil in the rain forest has few nutrients in it, some trees in this forest grow almost 200 feet (60 meters) tall. These trees get nutrients they need from decomposers. A special type of fungus gets its energy by breaking down the leaves that fall to the moist forest floor. The fungus connects to the roots of the trees, feeding nutrients from the decaying plant leaves directly to the trees.

The branches at the tops of these tall trees come together to form a canopy.

Many types of animals, such as monkeys, snakes, and birds, live in the canopy. They can get the food, water, and shelter they need in the treetops.

Animals of the tropical rain forest eat many different things. Hummingbirds, toucans, sloths, tapirs, monkeys, butterflies, beetles, and ants eat mostly fruit, bark, nectar, seeds, and leaves from plants. Other tropical rain forest animals, such as the praying mantis, jaguar, and boa constrictor, eat other animals.

The color and pattern of many animals help them blend in with the tropical rain forest. This protects them from predators. Some brightly colored parrots blend in with the brightly colored flowers and leaves in the tropical rain forest.

One animal, the sloth, blends in with the green plants because it has plants growing in its fur! The sloth spends most of its life hanging upside down in the trees, sleeping. Tiny algae plants grow in grooves on the sloth's hair, getting sunlight and rainfall while the sloth sleeps. The older a sloth gets, the greener its fur gets. Even more surprising are the moths that also live in the sloth's fur. These moths lay eggs in the sloth's hair. When the larvae hatch, they eat the algae.

The Salt Marsh

Along the coast, where the ocean meets the land, you can find salt marshes. Salt marshes are a kind of wetland. Once, people thought of these muddy, swampy-looking places as wastelands. Now most people know better. Salt marshes are rich with life. Many animals depend on salt marshes for food and shelter. In fact, many young animals grow up in salt marshes. They can find plenty of food and places to hide in the salt marshes. For this reason, some people call salt marshes the "nurseries of the sea."

The water in a salt marsh is a mixture of salt water (from the ocean) and freshwater (from the land). Only a few types of plants are able to grow in the salty mud. Special grasses and trees take the salty water up through their roots and push the salt crystals out through their leaves. They are able to change salt water into freshwater. These plants often cover the salt marsh.

At high tide, the ocean water comes in and covers the grasses. As the water becomes deeper, large fish swim into the area looking for smaller animals to eat. Small fish hide in the grasses from the bigger fish. Blue crabs use their claws to catch smaller fish and crabs.

Barnacles, mussels, clams, and scallops open their shells and filter microscopic plants and animals, called **plankton**, from the water. Snails, small crabs, and fish eat algae. Crabs and fish also eat dead plants and animals. Bacteria, so tiny that you cannot see them with the naked eye, break down dead plants and animals.

At low tide, the larger fish return to the ocean with the deep water. However, the marsh is still a busy place. The shallow water and exposed mud bottoms make it easy for land animals to find food. Wading birds, such as herons or egrets, walk along in search of tiny crabs and minnows. Other birds, such as owls, ospreys, pelicans, and red-winged blackbirds, fly over the marsh searching for smaller birds, insects, and fish to eat.

Raccoons break open the shells and eat the snails, clams, and crabs inside. Smaller fiddler crabs feed on the tiny bits of decaying plants and algae.

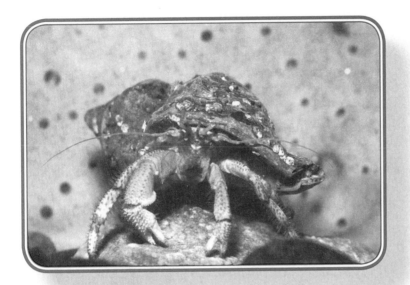

The plants and animals of the salt marsh are different because they live in salt water instead of freshwater. Some salt marsh animals hide among the grasses, while others burrow in the muddy bottom for shelter from the Sun and other animals. The color of many of the animals helps them blend in with the mud and water so predators can't find them easily.

Sharing Ideas

Read and discuss the following questions with your teammates. Then write your own response to each question in your notebook. Be prepared to share your responses with the class.

1. How are the producers in the salt marsh different from the producers in the forest? How are they the same?

2. How are the consumers in the tropical rain forest different from the consumers in the salt marsh? How are they the same?

3. How are the decomposers in the salt marsh different from the decomposers in your backyard? How are they the same?

4. How are producers, consumers, and decomposers connected in an ecosystem?

5. How are all living and nonliving things in all ecosystems—oak forest, tropical rain forest, and salt marsh—connected?

6. What are some of the important nonliving resources in all of the ecosystems?

7. What would happen if the producers—the trees, plants, or grasses—in an ecosystem disappeared?

Deepen Understanding through Vocabulary

1. Complete a "Concept Definition Map" for each of the following terms: producer, consumer, decomposer, and ecologist.

2. Add your charts to your notebook.

3. Be prepared to share your charts with the class.

Allen M. Young: An Ecologist

(1942–)

> What might a real-life ecologist do? What kind of problems might an ecologist solve? Read about a rain forest ecologist who unravels mysteries in a tropical rain forest. Complete the "Herringbone Graphic" as you read.

Who Is Dr. Young?

Dr. Allen Young solved a real-life mystery about a dazzling blue butterfly in a tropical rain forest! Dr. Young spent many years investigating and answering questions about the butterfly. He wanted to learn what this butterfly eats, its life cycle stages, and its habits in the wild. The more he learned, the more he wanted to know about the butterfly's interactions in its rain forest home.

What Did Dr. Young Do?

To observe the blue butterfly, Allen Young made his way through rivers, along jeep trails and slippery paths, and through the tangled trees and vines of the rain forests of Central America. As he traveled, he observed a food web that ties the blue butterfly to many living and nonliving things in this rain forest system.

What Did He Find Out?

Dr. Young discovered that the adult butterfly interacts with dead animals,

 rotting fruit, and fungi to obtain food. He observed that the fungi, in turn, depend on the butterfly to spread their reproductive spores. He also discovered that, as a caterpillar, the butterfly needs a special kind of plant, called the *Mucuna*, for food and shelter.

How Does the Mucuna Interact with Other Living Things?

While investigating the caterpillar, Allen Young observed interactions involving the *Mucuna* plant. He discovered that bats pollinated its flowers. He observed that animals such as tapirs, deer, peccaries, monkeys, agoutis, and squirrels ate the seedpods. The animals scattered the seeds so that new plants could grow in different places. He found out that flies and wasps ate the caterpillars that ate the *Mucuna*'s leaves.

Dr. Young observed that the *Mucuna* "climbed up" trunks of trees to reach sunlight needed to produce flowers.

He learned that this climbing interaction is harmful to some trees because the vines wrap around and "choke" the trees. But he also discovered one type of tree that is not harmed by the *Mucuna* plant's vines—the *Cecropia* tree.

The *Cecropia* tree is not harmed because it interacts with *Azteca* ants. The ants obtain food and shelter within the hollow trunk of the tree. In return, the ants use their sharp jaws to chew away the *Mucuna* vines that attempt to wrap around the *Cecropia* tree.

Why Is the Mucuna Important to the Rain Forest?

While studying the dazzling blue butterfly, Allen Young learned about the delicate balance of life in the tropical rain forest. For example, if the number of bats or decomposers suddenly decreases, the *Mucuna* plant might not be able to meet its needs and might experience a bad growing season.

When the *Mucuna* has a bad growing season, so do the butterflies, bats, and other things that depend on the *Mucuna* plants for food and shelter. On the other hand, if the number of wasps and flies that attack caterpillars increases, the *Mucuna* might have a good growing season because fewer of its leaves will be eaten by the caterpillars. However, if the wasps and flies eat more caterpillars, there will be fewer beautiful blue butterflies. If the number of *Cecropia* trees around a *Mucuna* increases, the *Mucuna* might not be able to reach the canopy to obtain the sunlight it needs to produce flowers. If the *Mucuna* plants cannot produce flowers, they cannot produce seeds and seedpods. If there are no seeds, there will be no new *Mucuna* plants. Everything really is connected to everything else!

Dr. Young believes that studying life in the rain forest is much like unraveling a mystery. Scientists work like detectives to find clues and information about the plants and animals and the ways they interact. But unlike storybook mysteries, the mystery of the dazzling blue butterfly might never be solved or completely understood. Many of the plants and animals in the tropical rain forests have not been discovered, studied, or named.

The mysteries that remain to be unraveled are as fascinating as those that have been discovered. The challenge for scientists like Allen Young is to observe and piece together the secrets of the rain forests while there still is time—before people change the rain forest ecosystem so much that it cannot recover.

✓ Checking Understanding

Part A: Each teammate will choose a different living thing (plant or animal) from an ecopicture. Talk about the following questions with your teammates. Then write your own response to each question in your notebook. Be prepared to share your responses with the class.

1. What is the name of your living thing?

2. Is your living thing a producer, consumer, or decomposer? Provide evidence to support your answer.

3. What interactions does your living thing experience to meet its need for food, water, shelter, and space? You may create either an interaction chart or a graphic organizer like the one of the mouse on page 74.

Part B: Review the "Doing Science" section on pages 1–19. Look at the graphic organizer on page 2. Talk about ways that you were doing science during this lesson. Then, on your own, describe ways in which you were doing science in your notebook.

Part C: Think about the activities that you did and the strategies that you used during this lesson. Talk about the following questions with your teammates. Then write your own response to each question in your notebook.

1. What did you learn during this lesson?

2. What activities or strategies helped you learn? How or why were they helpful?

3. Did working as a team help you learn? Why or why not?

4. What skills did your team do well? What skills does your team need to improve?

Lesson 5

Interactions in Your Own Backyard

You have been reading about interactions in different ecosystems. You have been observing the interactions in an ecosystem in your classroom and one near the school.

What interactions exist in your own backyard?
Read about a different backyard and find
out about the interactions that occur there.
Compare and contrast the following system with
a system that you have been observing on the
"Compare/Contrast Chart."

An Unusual Backyard

Where Is It? How Big Is It?

This "backyard" is 2,900 acres (1,160
hectares). It is on the western shore of
the Chesapeake Bay. (Before you read
further, find
the Chesapeake
Bay on a map
of the United
States.) This
big backyard
is the
Smithsonian
Environmental
Research
Center, called
SERC for short.

It is a large study system for many scientists. These scientists make it their business to know every tiny detail about the living things (animals and plants) and nonliving things (land, water, and air) in their study area. Scientists have been studying the interactions in this ecosystem for 40 years! The SERC study system contains forests, wetlands, creeks, rivers, abandoned fields, working farmland, and a salt marsh.

How Many Ecosystems Are There?

As you read in the last lesson, ecosystems can be different sizes. The entire 2,900 acres of the SERC study system can be considered one ecosystem. The study system can also be divided into parts. It contains forests, fields, farmland, rivers, and salt marshes.

All of these places are different sizes. They contain different things. But all of the places contain living and nonliving things. Remember that the living things in all ecosystems can be classified as producers, consumers, and decomposers. In all ecosystems, the living things interact with each other and nonliving things to get energy, to survive, and to grow.

What Do the Scientists Look For?

Over the past 40 years, SERC scientists have poked, prodded, and measured the land, water, and air. They have learned many things about forest and salt marsh ecosystems. However, there are more clues to uncover and much more to learn.

The clues to how nature works are often difficult to uncover because the clues are found where people normally are strangers. Clues can be found deep under the ground, at the bottom of the salt marsh, and in the tallest part of the forest.

What Have Scientists Learned?

All the time, SERC scientists are learning more about how ecosystems work. Then they use what they learn to solve "real-world" problems. Here are some examples:

- At the SERC site, scientists study what happens to a raindrop that falls from the sky onto plant leaves. Learning about the process of how plants interact with raindrops helps them understand what happens to tree leaves when they interact with chemicals found in raindrops.

- The SERC scientists uncover clues and find patterns that tell about the health of forests. Understanding patterns allows scientists to see early warning signs of unhealthy interactions, such as drought or insect invasions.

- The scientists investigate what happens when "stowaway" organisms from foreign places arrive in the ecosystem. To do this, scientists study ballast water. Ballast water is the water that is put in the bottom of ships to keep the ships steady at sea.

When an empty ship arrives in the port, members of the ship's crew empty its ballast water into the Chesapeake Bay before they load the ship with cargo. The ballast water can be from foreign places like the Indian Ocean or the Mediterranean Sea. When the foreign ballast water empties into the Chesapeake Bay, a whole aquarium of creatures is released into the ecosystem of the bay. Scientists study what happens when a new type of organism is introduced into the ecosystem. What does it eat? What eats it? Does it have any natural predators in its new environment?

- SERC scientists investigate the chain of events that starts when fertilizer from a farm field enters the salt marsh, causing sea grass to die. Scientists know that this event also will affect the blue crabs and other animals in the salt marsh because they depend on sea grass to survive.

- Scientists study the interactions of blue crabs with other living and nonliving things. To do this, the scientists strap sound-emitting devices, which look something like little backpacks, onto the crabs so that the scientists can track the crabs' activities. Scientists want to learn more about the crabs' feeding interactions, movement, molting, and fighting behavior. Learning about the habits of the blue crab will allow scientists to understand how commercial fishing might affect the blue crab population.

There are few backyards that have been this closely studied by scientists for such a long time. Even so, the SERC scientists say they have a lot to learn about what goes on in this huge ecosystem—their study system. Every day, they learn something new that helps them better understand this ecosystem and the relationships between living and nonliving things in ecosystems in general.

Showing the Interactions in Your Study Systems

What has been happening in your study systems? Have you found interactions like those the SERC scientists have found at their site near the Chesapeake Bay? Your notebook is your written record of what you have observed. You will use the information in your notebook to show interactions in your study systems (or one of your study systems), just as scientists do.

■ Team Task

List the living and nonliving things found in one of your study systems. Draw an ecopicture of the study system. Then show the interactions between living and nonliving things in that ecosystem. Explain what happens between the living and nonliving things.

■ Team Jobs

Materials Manager   Tracker   Messenger

■ Team Skills

Listen when others talk.

■ Team Supplies

- 3 pieces of chart paper
- each teammate's notebook
- markers or crayons
- 3 pencils
- 3 wristbands

Directions

1. With your teammates, compare your notebook notes about one of your study systems.

   a. How are your observations the same?

   b. How are your observations different?

2. List the living and nonliving things in your study system. Did you include the Sun?

Listen to one another. Let each teammate suggest something for the team's poster.

3. On your first sheet of chart paper, create a team ecopicture that shows all the living and nonliving things in your study system.

4. On your second sheet of chart paper, create a chart like the following one. Classify all the living things in your study system as producers, consumers, or decomposers.

Producers	Consumers	Decomposers

5. Label your third sheet of chart paper "Interactions." Draw or describe interactions for food, water, shelter, or space that you observed in your study system. Make sure that you provide at least one example for each need.

6. Be prepared to share your charts with the class.

Ask questions of your teammates if you are not sure about certain interactions or if you do not agree with what is on the poster.

Sharing Ideas

Compare each team's ecopicture, classification chart, and interactions.

1. How are they the same?

2. How are they different?

✓ Checking Understanding

Part A: Observe your school-yard ecosystem. Talk about the following questions with your teammates. Then write your own response to each question in your notebook. Be prepared to share your responses with the class.

1. What interactions between living and nonliving things have you observed in your school-yard ecosystem?

2. How could you improve your school-yard ecosystem for plants and animals?

Part B: Review the "Doing Science" section on pages 1–19. Look at the graphic organizer on page 2. Talk about ways that you were doing science during this lesson. Then, on your own, describe ways in which you were doing science in your notebook.

Part C: Think about the activities that you did and the strategies that you used during this lesson. Talk about the following questions with your teammates. Then write your own response to each question in your notebook.

1. What did you learn during this lesson?

2. What activities or strategies helped you learn? How or why were they helpful?

3. Did working as a team help you learn? Why or why not?

4. What skills did your team do well? What skills does your team need to improve?

Lesson 6

Oh Deer!

Have you ever seen a deer? You could probably see one if you visited a salt marsh or an oak forest. Deer often come into open meadow areas to find food. Do you think they might interact with the grass and other plants in the meadow area?

Sharing Ideas

When the game is over, look at the class data and talk about these questions with your classmates.

1. What happened to the size of the deer herd when there was plenty of food, water, shelter, and space?

2. What happened to the size of the deer herd when there was a limited amount of food, water, shelter, or space?

3. In a real forest, what do you think would happen to the size of a deer herd when resources were plentiful? What about when resources were scarce?

4. In a real forest, with what resources would the deer interact to meet their needs for food, water, shelter, and space?

5. In a real forest, what might cause the amount of food, water, shelter, or space to change from year to year?

6. Besides birth or death, what else might cause the size of a deer herd to change?

On Your Own

Graphing the Data

Your class counted and recorded the number of deer in the herd after each round of the game. These numbers, or data, can help you understand the relationship between the size of a deer herd and the interactions with available resources in the forest. Just looking at the numbers might not tell you much. A better way to understand the data is to plot the data points on a graph. A graph can help you see patterns in the data.

■ *Your Task*

Draw a line graph of the data from the Oh Deer! game. In your notebook, describe any patterns you find in the data. Be ready to share your graph and any pattern you find.

■ *Your Supplies*

- 1 ruler
- 1 sheet of graph paper
- your notebook
- 1 marker or crayon
- 1 pencil

Directions

1. If you do not know how to make a line graph, work with your teacher and read "How to Make a Line Graph" on pages 136–144.

2. On your graph paper, draw and label the axes of your graph.

   a. The horizontal scale shows the number of years.

   b. The vertical scale shows the number of deer.

3. Number the scales on your graph.

   a. Number the horizontal scale (the years) from 0 to the number of rounds the class played the game.

   b. Number the vertical scale (the number of deer) from 0 to the number of students who played the game.

Your graph should look something like the following.

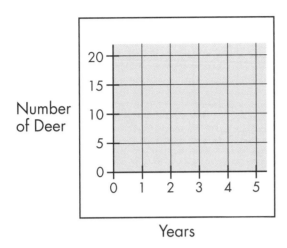

4. For each year (each round of the game), mark a dot that shows the number of deer the class counted in the herd at the end of that year.

   a. This is called "plotting the points" on your graph.

   b. Your graph should show one point for each year (each round) of the game.

5. Draw a line that connects all the points on your graph.

Ask for help from a teammate if you are not sure how to plot the points on your graph.

Your graph might look something like the
following.

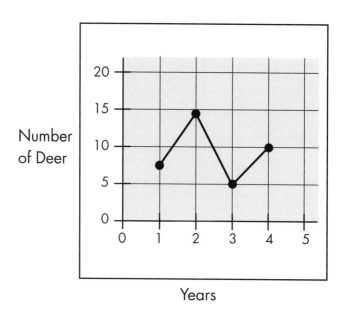

Number
of Deer

Years

Do you see any
patterns in the
data?

6. Describe in your notebook what you think the
graph shows.

Ideas to Think About

Meet with your team and talk about answers
to the following questions. Use the data from
your graph to answer the questions. Write the
answers in your own notebook.

1. What is the largest number of deer that
survived for one year in this forest? Why were
there so many deer?

2. What happened to the size of the deer herd the year after the herd was at its largest?

3. What is the smallest number of deer that survived for one year in this forest? Why were there so few deer?

4. What happened to the size of the deer herd the year after the herd was at its smallest?

5. Why does the pattern on your graph go up and down instead of remaining in a straight line like the following graph?

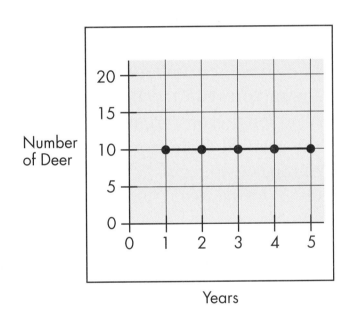

How to Make a Line Graph

A. Graphs are a way to display data so that you can look for patterns. All graphs have several things in common. First, graphs have a horizontal (side to side) line called the horizontal axis and a vertical (up and down) line called the vertical axis. These lines are the **axes** of the graph. ("Axes" is the plural of the word "axis.") The point where the two axes meet is the **zero point**, or the point where the graph begins. Both lines have a number scale marked on them. You read the horizontal scale from left (zero) to right. You read the vertical scale from bottom (zero) to top.

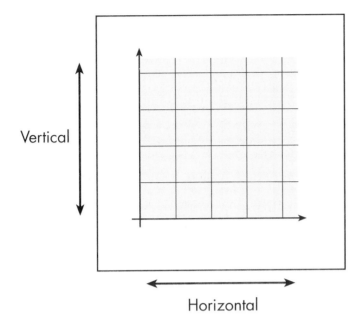

Vertical

Horizontal

B. The number scale on one axis does not have to be exactly the same as the number scale on the other axis, but the difference between the numbers on any one axis must be the same. For example, in the following graph, the difference between the numbers next to each other on the horizontal axis is one. In other words, you count by ones along the horizontal axis. The difference between the numbers next to each other on the vertical axis is two, so you count by twos to set up the vertical number scale.

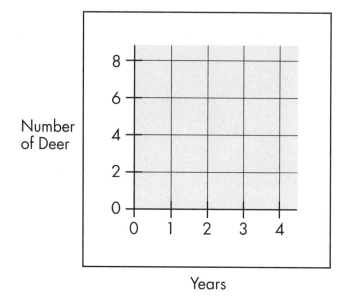

On any number scale, you can count by threes, by tens, or even by one hundreds. The important thing is to keep the same difference between the numbers along the scale. Your data will help you decide whether to count by twos, by fives, or by one hundreds, depending on how large your numbers on the graph need to be.

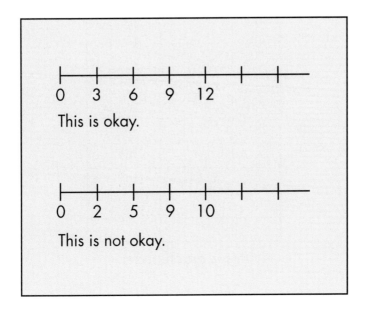

This is okay.

This is not okay.

Using graph paper will help you set up a proper number scale. Graph paper is a special kind of paper that has lines evenly drawn on it. Because the distance between each line is the same, graph paper helps you show that the difference is equal between numbers next to each other on the scale.

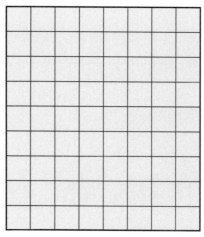

This is graph paper.

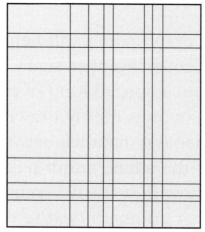

This is not graph paper.

C. To make a line graph, first you have to plot the data points. This means that you will make a dot at the place where the data point on the horizontal axis matches the data point on the vertical axis. Read the following example to find out how to do this.

The following illustration is an outline of a graph that will show how much a bean plant grew in five weeks.

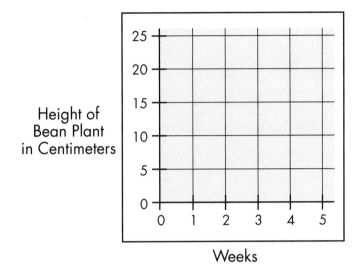

Height of Bean Plant in Centimeters

Weeks

The student who did this investigation recorded these data.

Weeks	Height of Bean Plant in Centimeters
1	5
2	8
3	10
4	20
5	22

At the end of the first week, the plant was 5 centimeters (2 inches) tall. To find this point on the graph, put one finger on the correct number for the week (week 1) on the horizontal axis. Put another finger on the correct height in centimeters (5 centimeters) on the vertical axis. Move your two fingers together until they meet. Then make a dot at the place where your two fingers meet. You have just plotted your first data point!

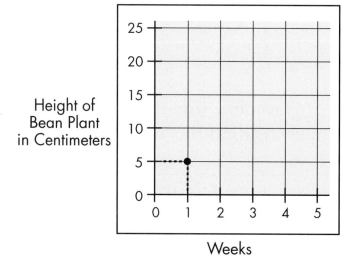

By the end of the second week, the plant was 8 centimeters (3 inches) tall. Eight centimeters is not a number on the vertical axis, but you know that 8 is between 5 and 10.

Therefore, you can estimate where 8 centimeters would be on the vertical axis. Put one finger on the vertical axis where 8 centimeters should be; put another finger on the horizontal axis for week 2. Move your fingers together and draw a dot where they meet. This is the second data point.

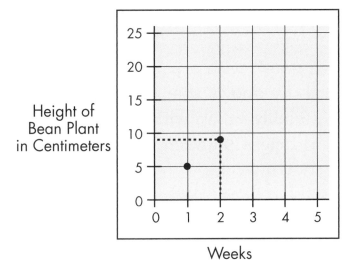

After you plot all the data points, use a ruler to draw a line that connects the data points in order.

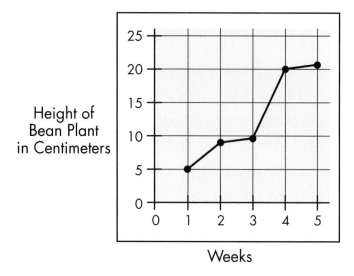

Height of
Bean Plant
in Centimeters

Weeks

A graph with a pattern like the one above shows that the bean plant got steadily taller, with a large increase in height between the third and fourth weeks.

What would a graph with a pattern like the following show?

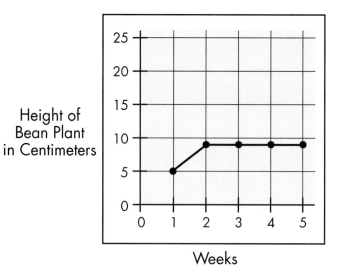

Height of
Bean Plant
in Centimeters

Weeks

Deer in Winter

When winter arrives, you turn up the thermostat and make hot chocolate. Winter can bring hardship to wild animals, however. Deer wade through deep snow to find a dinner of dry twigs.

They shiver on cold nights while you watch television and eat popcorn. The furnace that keeps you warm is in your basement. Deer must make their own heat—and keep it inside.

All furnaces need fuel. Your house may be heated by oil, propane, natural gas, wood, or electricity. Deer must get their heat from calories in food. Calories are fuel for deer. *Forage* (food) is scarce in winter, so deer must work hard to get enough calories to keep body temperature up. The struggle to find food burns calories too.

The Layered Look

Two-layer winter coats help deer save calories and stay warm. There's a woolly undercoat and an outer covering of hollow guard hairs that trap and hold body heat. Deer shed their guard hairs in spring. The woolly undercoat breaks up slowly in summer, to be replaced by a new one in fall, when new guard hairs begin to grow. The fall and winter coat of most deer is gray or nut-brown. In spring and summer, deer appear almost red.

Deer lose weight when they have to struggle through snow to find food. Adult deer can lose as much as one-third of their weight without suffering harm. If you lost that much, you'd probably be very thin and hungry! That's what often happens to fawns in winter. Like kids, fawns are a lot smaller than adults.

They can't afford to lose as much weight. When fawns lose one-third of their weight, they rarely survive.

A *doe* (female deer) carrying a *fetus* (unborn fawn) may lose it during a hard winter. This is nature's way of making sure that one animal survives, even if it means losing another.

As new plants and tree buds grow in spring, deer eat what they want. They choose healthful, high-calorie foods called "ice-cream" forage. Deer do fine then. The weather is mild, and living is easier with a lot of high-energy food around. Fawns drinking their mother's milk have the richest diet of all. When a doe is producing milk, she needs more than twice as many calories as a deer that is not nursing a baby.

Deer Spinach

After they have gained back lost body weight, deer begin putting on fat to help them make it through the next winter. They choose food not just for taste but for nutrition (you too probably have to eat things that aren't exactly your favorite food—like spinach or broccoli, just because it's good for you). Different plants have different amounts of fat. Dry grass has hardly any, while juicy shrubs are full of it.

Good-Bye, Good Stuff

When winter arrives, diet changes. Gone are the mushrooms and delicate *forbs* (small, tender plants such as wild strawberries). When snow gets deep, deer can't move far or reach buried food. They start eating "survival" food like fir needles and lichens. Deer even eat dry thistles if they have to.

Deer seek out places where Sun and wind keep snow from piling up. But you'll also find them on cold north slopes. Can you guess why? The reason is that more trees grow on north slopes. The tree branches catch snow and keep it from piling up on the ground so that deer don't have to struggle through it looking for food.

Places that stay cool in winter also keep snow soft. Snow that melts, then freezes again, forms a hard crust that cuts deer's legs. Coyotes and dogs can run on top of a snow crust and catch deer, whose sharp hooves break through. Dogs—even small ones—can kill many deer in winter if they're allowed to run loose.

Deer Yards

In the West, about Thanksgiving time, mule deer migrate from the mountains to lowlands where snow isn't as deep and there is more food. In the Northeast, white-tailed deer *yard up* (gather) in swamps and woodlands where trees break the wind and where their own travel keeps trails open for a little way around the yard. If deer eat the forage around the deer yard before spring, they may starve. In a really harsh winter, they get so weak and thin that they die even after the spring grasses begin to grow. They've just lost too much energy to survive.

Hard Decisions

Sometimes state wildlife workers and other concerned people feed deer to help them through the worst of the winter months. If deer learn to expect handouts, they become *dependent* (unable to take care of themselves). Whenever possible, it's best for humans not to tamper with nature. By feeding deer instead of letting nature take its course, people often find that they've made matters worse. If there is a harsh winter again next year, all those deer that humans saved from starvation will be competing with other deer for food.

Sippin' and Thinkin'

While you sip your hot chocolate in cozy comfort, think about deer and their ways of surviving winter. And if you go walking in the deer's snowy world, take it easy, go softly. Try not to startle the wild creatures or cause them to run. They need every bit of their energy just to stay alive.

Part A: Talk about the following questions with your teammates. Then write your own response to each question in your notebook. Be prepared to share your responses with the class.

1. In what ways do deer interact with other living and nonliving things to obtain food, water, shelter, and space?

2. How are interactions influenced by changes in the seasons?

Part B: Review the "Doing Science" section on pages 1–19. Look at the graphic organizer on page 2. Talk about ways that you were doing science during this lesson. Then, on your own, describe ways in which you were doing science in your notebook.

Part C: Think about the activities that you did and the strategies that you used during this lesson. Talk about the following questions with your teammates. Then write your own response to each question in your notebook.

1. What did you learn during this lesson?

2. What activities or strategies helped you learn? How or why were they helpful?

3. Did working as a team help you learn? Why or why not?

4. What skills did your team do well? What skills does your team need to improve?

Lesson 7

Trees Have Interactions Too!

Like animals, trees have needs and interactions. However, trees are stuck where they grow. They cannot move like animals. What do trees need to survive? How can trees get their needs met to survive if they can't move? Trees experience all kinds of interactions, both from living and nonliving things.

A Tree's Interactions

Interactions for Water

Trees need water to survive. When there is enough rain, trees get as much water as they need to grow. When there are droughts—periods when no or very little

rain falls—there is no water at or near the surface of the earth. During times of drought, a tree's roots grow deeper until they reach water supplies farther underground. The roots of many trees intertwine as the trees compete for the limited supply of water. Trees interact with other trees—living things—and with rain and underground water supplies—nonliving things—to survive.

Interactions for Sunlight

Trees also need energy from sunlight to make their own food. Sometimes trees have to compete for sunlight. Shorter trees growing in forests where the

larger trees block most of the sunlight sometimes bend to reach the sunlight. In this way, trees interact with other trees—living things—and with sunlight, a nonliving thing—to grow and survive.

Interactions for Space

Trees need space to grow. When one tree falls, other trees grow in the space the original tree once occupied. The leaves of some kinds of trees have chemicals that wash out after their leaves fall to the ground.

These chemicals prevent other kinds of trees from growing in that place. Therefore, only new trees of the same kind can grow in that area. In this way, trees compete with other trees for the space they need to grow and survive.

Other Kinds of Interactions

Another nonliving thing with which trees interact is the wind. Some trees depend on the wind to scatter their seeds, so that some seeds will land away from the parent trees. In this way, the new trees might have more space and a better chance of getting their needs met. The wind also blows pollen from tree to tree so that the trees can produce new seeds.

Some interactions between trees and animals are helpful for the trees. For example, some trees produce rough and jagged seeds that stick to an animal's fur, in the mud on an animal's feet, or on the clothing of people who brush against the plants.

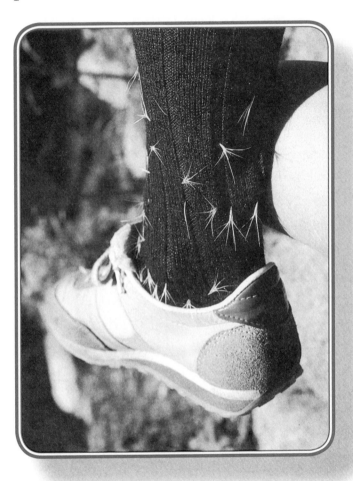

Then animals can carry a tree's seeds to places where there might be more space for a new tree to grow.

On the other hand, some interactions between trees and animals harm the trees. For example, when insects chew on the leaves or bark of trees, the trees cannot swat at the pests or run away. Trees just have to stand there.

Some trees, like the balsam fir, make chemicals that stop the growth of insects. Other trees have large thorns that protect  them from munching animals. Trees without such protection might have their leaves eaten and their bark stripped by hungry animals. These types of interactions can kill the trees or keep them from growing very much.

Look at the following photograph. Does it show helpful or harmful interactions for the tree? Why do you think so?

Interactions and Growth

Interactions affect how much, or how little, trees grow each year. Good interactions promote a good growing season. During a good growing season, a tree's interactions allow it to get all the energy from sunlight, the space, and the water that it needs. When a tree's needs are met, it can grow taller and bigger around.

Bad interactions could be insect attacks, drought, or fire. These make it difficult for trees to get their needs met. If they don't get all the energy they need from sunlight, the space, and the water, they are unable to grow very much.

Recorded in Rings

Trees keep records of their interactions in their yearly growth rings. Each year, as a tree grows bigger around, it adds two layers of wood around its trunk. One layer is light. One layer is dark. Together, these layers of wood form a tree ring.

If you look at a slice of a tree trunk, you will see that the layers of wood form a pattern of tree rings. Each ring represents one season's growth. In the spring, when the tree grows rapidly, the tree adds the light-colored layer. Later in the summer, tree growth slows down. At this time, the tree adds a darker-colored layer.

Because most trees make one ring each year, you can tell how old a tree is by counting its rings. Since trees get thicker as they get older, the oldest ring is in the center of the tree; the youngest ring is right under the bark.

Oldest Ring

Youngest Ring

Tree rings also tell about the history of the tree. The width of each ring tells whether the year was a good one or a bad one for the tree. A wide ring shows that the tree had a good growing season. The tree's interactions helped it meet its needs. In that year, the tree grew a lot! A narrow ring means that the tree

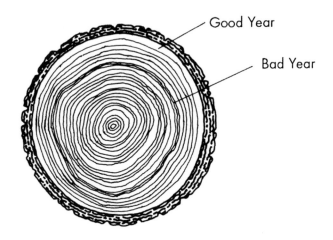

Good Year

Bad Year

experienced a bad year and did not grow very much. Maybe interactions with other trees or with the environment did not allow the tree to get the sunlight or water that it needed to grow.

Sometimes tree rings show scars. The scars may be a tree's record of a limb that broke off after a heavy snow. Scars might be evidence of a fire that swept through the forest. Scars might show there were burrowing insects or some other kind of interaction that caused injury to the tree.

A tree even records information about where it was growing. By examining tree rings, you can tell if a tree was growing on a hillside or on flat land. You can also tell if a tree was leaning to one side. Perhaps the tree did not have the space it needed to grow straight up. Perhaps a rock or another tree or plant was crowding its space.

How do you get a slice of a tree trunk to study? It's easy if someone has already cut the tree down to make firewood or lumber. Then you can just saw a slice off a log. If the tree is still standing, however, you have to chop down the tree to see a slice of the trunk. Would that be a helpful or harmful interaction for the tree?

Scientists use a method called **coring** to study a tree's growth rings without killing the tree. They use a special drill to bore into the trunk of a standing tree and remove a piece of wood about the size of a straw. The growth rings show up as lines on the core sample.

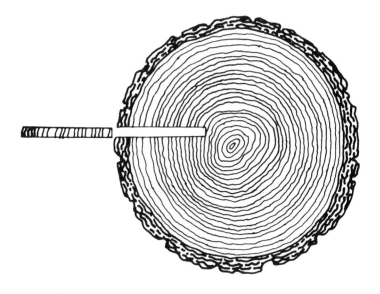

Examining a Tree's Interactions

In this activity, you and your teammates will study a slice of a tree trunk. The team will find out how old the tree was when it was cut down, its best growth year, its worst growth year, and what might have caused growth differences. Later in this lesson, you each will write a story that describes what a year in the life of this tree might have been like.

■ *Team Task*

Describe everything you can about the history of one tree. Brainstorm a list of interactions that could have occurred in the tree's lifetime. List reasons why the tree might have grown the way it did in both its best year and its worst year.

■ *Team Jobs*

Materials Manager

Tracker

Messenger

■ *Team Skills*

Discuss many ideas before selecting one.

Team Supplies

- 1 cross section of a tree (Use the illustration on page 170 or the real sample your teacher gives you.)

- 1 ruler

- 3 hand lenses

- each teammate's notebook

- 3 pencils

- 3 wristbands

- 1 plastic tray

Directions

1. Record how old this tree was when it was cut down.

2. Find the ring that shows the tree's best year.

   a. Measure it as accurately as possible.

   b. Record the width of the ring.

   c. Record the age of the tree when it made this ring.

3. Find the ring that shows the tree's worst year.

   a. Measure it as accurately as possible.

   b. Record the width of the ring.

   c. Record the age of the tree when it made this ring.

4. Brainstorm and record a list of interactions that could have caused the tree to grow as much as it did in its best year.

5. Brainstorm and record another list of interactions that could have caused the tree to grow as little as it did in its worst year.

6. On each list, circle the three interactions that you think most likely caused the tree to grow the way it did.

Look for evidence of interactions such as insect holes, a fire scar, or other scarring.

How to Brainstorm

A. State any idea that comes to your mind.

B. Record everyone's ideas. Don't judge whether the ideas are good or bad.

C. Keep thinking of ideas for at least five minutes.

D. If you can't think of an idea, look at something already on the list. Try to add something to that idea or change the idea slightly.

Part B: Review the "Doing Science" section on pages 1–19. Look at the graphic organizer on page 2. Talk about ways that you were doing science during this lesson. Then, on your own, describe ways in which you were doing science in your notebook.

Part C: Think about the activities that you did and the strategies that you used during this lesson. Talk about the following questions with your teammates. Then write your own response to each question in your notebook.

1. What did you learn during this lesson?

2. What activities or strategies helped you learn? How or why were they helpful?

3. Did working as a team help you learn? Why or why not?

4. What skills did your team do well? What skills does your team need to improve?

 Lesson 8

Back and Forth in Ecosystems

> *When we try to pick out something by itself, we find it hitched to everything else in the universe.*
> —John Muir, Naturalist (1838–1914)

What does the above statement mean to you?

How does this statement relate to what you have learned in this module? What examples do you see of things being "hitched" to one another in the ecosystem shown in the picture on page 173?

Finding the Balance

What happens when the amount of a resource, such as food, changes in an ecosystem? As you found out when you played the game of Oh Deer, a change in a resource affects the plants and animals that need that resource. What do these graphs tell you about changes in the deer population from one year to the next?

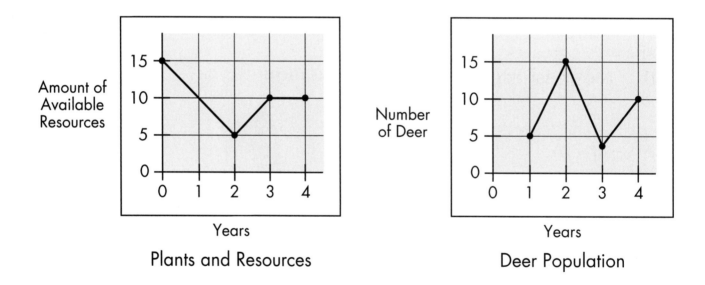

The graphs above show how the size of the deer population changed as the amount of resources in the forest ecosystem changed.

The number of deer that could live in the forest was balanced by the amount of available food, water, shelter, and space. When too many deer were in the forest one year, they used up the resources and fewer deer could survive the next year. After the number of deer decreased, the forest's resources could recover. Then there were more resources to support a larger deer population again. In a healthy ecosystem, there is a constant give and take between populations of plants and animals and the resources they need to survive.

When an ecosystem is in balance, the numbers of plants and animals change constantly, sometimes up and sometimes down, when resources become abundant or scarce. The highest and lowest points on the graph show the greatest and fewest numbers of deer that the forest could support. As long as the deer herd remains within these numbers, the ecosystem remains balanced, even if the balance shifts slightly each year.

Can ecosystems ever become unbalanced? What changes might upset the balance in an ecosystem?

Changes in the Ecosystems

Changes constantly happen in ecosystems. Most of the time, the changes are small and expected, such as changes in the seasons, in the weather, in the amount of light and rainfall, and in the numbers of specific plants and animals that are born and die.

Some changes have much greater effects on ecosystems, however. Nature causes some of the large changes. Volcanoes, fires, and landslides are a few of the ways that nature causes big changes in ecosystems.

Some changes in ecosystems are caused by people. For example, filling in a salt marsh or a wetland area to make room for houses would be a large change caused by people. Instead of interactions between birds, fish, sea grasses, and salt water, new interactions between people, lawns, flowers, trees, and automobiles would begin in that location. The change would be too large to keep the balance in the original ecosystem.

Studying day-to-day interactions helps scientists understand what might happen when large changes happen within an ecosystem. Which living things might be hurt and which might be helped by the change? Being able to predict the effects of such changes on an ecosystem is important for making decisions about managing ecosystems. Foresters, wildlife experts, and ecologists study changes in ecosystems so that all of us can make better decisions about taking care of our planet Earth.

Read about changes to three ecosystems caused by nature and by people. What types of changes help or harm ecosystems? When should people step in and try to stop the changes from happening? What would you decide?

Ecosystem Change #1:
A Fire in Yellowstone!

The summer of 1988 was hot and dry across all the United States. The dry conditions were especially bad in the western United States. Farmers and ranchers lost many crops and livestock because of the **drought**. A drought is a long period of time with very little or no rain. Everything was really dry!

Park rangers in Yellowstone National Park in Wyoming knew that the drought had made the park very dry and that the danger of a forest fire was high. However, the park rangers weren't too worried.

They knew that even though fires are dangerous, they can be good for parts of the park's ecosystem. Fires return nutrients to the soil, open up the forest so that more light can get to the forest floor, and allow new plants to grow, which make extra food for the animals.

Rangers usually let nature take its course. They let fires that start naturally, by lightning strikes, for example, burn naturally and go out on their own. Those fires usually burn only a few acres, which helps keep the forest ecosystem in balance. The rangers only fight the fires that people start or that threaten campgrounds or areas of the park used by visitors. This "natural burn" policy often is hard for park visitors to understand because most people think of forest fires as bad. Park visitors think that scorched trees and grasslands are ugly.

The conditions in 1988 were a problem, however, for a couple of reasons. First, it was extremely dry with no rain in the forecast. Second, for the last several years, very few natural fires had started in Yellowstone National Park. Because of this, dead leaves and twigs covered the forest floor. All this fuel could make the next fire a hot one!

That summer, lightning strikes started fires in several parts of the dry park. To add to the problem, careless woodcutters and campers accidentally started other fires outside the park boundary that spread inside the park. Because of the dry conditions, the fires quickly spread.

At first, the rangers followed their natural burn policy. They let the lightning fires burn, but fought the fires started by people. But the dry ground, hot temperatures, and wind made all the fires spread. The rangers decided to fight all the fires this time. They brought in thousands of firefighters, hundreds of fire engines, and dozens of helicopters. They used bulldozers to cut miles of firebreaks and spent millions of dollars trying to stop the fires with chemicals and water. Nothing seemed to work.

The fires burned all summer until the first snowfall finally brought moisture to the park. When the fires were over, rangers and scientists inspected the damage to the plants and animals. One million acres (400,000 hectares) burned.

Over half the area had burned all the way to the treetops and killed all the older trees. In the rest of the burned area, the fire had remained cooler and stayed close to the ground. The trees in those areas were scorched but still alive.

Many of the small animals, such as snakes and crawling insects, died in the fires. Surprisingly, only small numbers of large animals, such as elk, bison, moose, and bear, died in the fires. Most were able to run out of the burning woods to safer areas.

The problem for the large animals came during the following cold, snowy winter. The temperatures were especially cold that winter. Food was scarce because much of the plant life had died during the drought. Plants that were left had been burned during the fire. Large numbers of elk and bison died. The numbers of dying elk shocked the winter visitors to the park.

The visitors asked the park rangers to bring in food for the elk so they would survive the winter. The rangers refused and again thought it best to let nature take its course. They said that feeding the animals works against nature because the animals stop looking for food on their own. The animals then would stay only in one small area. This damages the area and allows disease to spread among the animals.

After examining the dead elk, the park rangers observed that most were old, without teeth, and thin. Those elk had survived this long because the winters before had been mild. The rangers wrote in their report, "This is not a zoo. It's a national park, where the death of one animal means life to another."

Elk that are weak and dying in the spring will help get the new crop of grizzly bear cubs off to a good start in life."

Although they hurt the elk herd, the fires and the cold, snowy winter helped other animals in Yellowstone, such as eagles, ravens, magpies, coyotes, and grizzly bears. These animals fed on the dead bodies of the winter-killed animals. They had plenty of food to eat, and their populations grew.

In the spring and summer, the burned areas in the park became carpeted with grasses and wildflowers. Some of the seeds blew in from unburned areas. Others were carried on the fur of animals or in animal droppings. Still other seeds were in the soil before the fires occurred, waiting years in some cases for the flood of sunshine that followed the fire.

Tiny tree seedlings began to grow out of the ashes. For the most part, Yellowstone's forests, grasses, and wildflowers replanted themselves, just as they had done all through history. Beetles and other insects laid eggs in the burned tree snags. When the eggs hatched, woodpeckers, mountain bluebirds, robins, and other birds flew in from all over to feast on the young insects.

Today lodgepole pine seedlings continue to grow. Plants and animals continue to prosper. Scientists and rangers will continue to study Yellowstone National Park and its changes.

Ecosystem Change #2: Ocean Hunters

At one time, Pacific sea otters lived off the west coast of North America. They lived in beds of giant seaweed, called kelp. Every year thousands of otters were killed by hunters for their fur. By the early 1900s, almost no sea otters were left. As the sea otters disappeared, people noticed that something was happening to the beds of kelp, the eagles, the harbor seals, and many fish. They were disappearing too! What was happening?

Kelp is the green plant at the beginning of many ocean food chains. It is eaten by tiny animals that are eaten by bigger animals that are eaten by fishes. The fishes are food for eagles and seals, as well as people. Kelp also is eaten by spiny creatures called sea urchins.

As the sea urchins feed on the kelp, they often cut off the kelp stems at the seafloor. The kelp then floats away. It just so happens that sea urchins are one of the sea otters' favorite foods. Does this give you a clue as to why the kelp, eagles, harbor seals, and fishes disappeared when the otters were hunted and killed?

Because everything is connected to everything else, when hunters killed the sea otters, there were no animals left to eat the sea urchins. The number of

sea urchins grew and grew until they destroyed the kelp beds. When the kelp beds were destroyed, the animals that fed on kelp had no food, and the animals that fed on the animals that fed on kelp had no food. Do you see the pattern here?

Once scientists and citizens realized what was happening, they put a stop to the hunting of sea otters before all the sea otters were destroyed. Then the number of sea otters began to increase. As the sea otters found their favorite food, the sea urchins, the number of sea urchins decreased. This helped the kelp beds grow back. When the kelp supply was renewed, the fishes and other animals came back to feed on the kelp. When the fishes came back, so did the eagles and the harbor seals. What do you think might have happened if all the sea otters had been hunted for their fur?

Ecosystem Change #3:
Something Is Fishy in Yellowstone Lake

In July 1994, a fishing guide brought a 19-inch (48-centimeter) lake trout to show park rangers. The big fish was an alien species. It was not a natural part of the Yellowstone Lake ecosystem. Soon, more and more people were catching lake trout. Where had they come from? How did they get into the lake?

"It's an appalling act of environmental vandalism," the superintendent of the park reported. No one knew *who* put the fish in the lake. No one knew *when* the fish were put into the lake. No one knew *how many* lake trout were put in the lake. But one thing the park rangers did know—big changes in Yellowstone Lake's food web were going to happen.

Because they understood the connections in the lake's ecosystem, scientists knew that the alien lake trout would cause many changes to the natural ecosystem. The "environmental vandals," who illegally released the fish, probably did not realize that the new fish would harm the lake ecosystem. They had not learned that everything in nature is connected to everything else! The people who put the lake trout into the lake might have thought they were helping other people who like to catch fish. But, introducing a type of animal that is not natural to an ecosystem can cause many unexpected changes!

The first change scientists observed was a change in the food chain within the lake. Scientists predicted that the alien lake trout would eat, and eat, and eat the natural cutthroat trout. A lake trout can grow very large, up to 60 pounds (27 kilograms)! A cutthroat trout weighs only about 3 pounds (about 1.5 kilograms). The lake trout would probably devour their little cousins until few remained.

Cutthroat trout have lived in Yellowstone Lake for thousands of years and have not been eaten by other fish. Therefore, there have been large numbers of cutthroat trout in the lake. Plenty of cutthroats have been available for wildlife and those who like to fish. All this has changed. In other places where lake trout have been introduced into a lake ecosystem, they have eaten the natural fish population until none remained.

Because everything in an ecosystem is connected, there will be other changes in the food web. In the natural ecosystem, cutthroat trout live in shallow lake water and in the streams that feed into the lake. They are the food for at least 42 different kinds of birds and mammals, including ospreys, bald eagles, coyotes, ravens, deer, mice, and grizzly bears. These animals depend on the cutthroat trout as a food source. Ospreys, in fact, eat almost nothing but cutthroat trout.

The alien lake trout cannot serve as food for the birds and mammals for several reasons. The alien lake trout live in deep water, often as deep as 150 feet (26 meters). This is too deep for the birds and mammals to reach them. Also, because the lake trout do not live in the streams that feed into the lake, they are not available to grizzly bears, otters, and other kinds of animals that feed in the rivers. A report stated that "the Yellowstone cutthroat trout is the central, or keystone, species in the Yellowstone Lake ecosystem, and its decline or disappearance would have disastrous consequences for much of the remaining animal life."

To lower the number of lake trout, the park service has asked those who fish to hook as many lake trout as they can and not to throw them back into the lake. The U.S. Fish and Wildlife Service began experimenting to discover how best to keep the number of lake trout low without harming the cutthroat trout. They recommended netting the lake trout to limit population growth. The program, though, will cost almost $9 million over the next 30 years.

Sharing Ideas

Get together with your teammates from the last lesson. Decide which teammate will analyze "Ecosystem Change #1," "Ecosystem Change #2," and "Ecosystem Change #3." Each teammate will answer the questions only about that story. Write your answers in your notebook. Share and discuss your team's answers. Then compare your ideas with those of your classmates.

Ecosystem Change #1: A Fire in Yellowstone!

1. What are some of the interactions that were changed by the Yellowstone fire?

2. Which plants and animals were helped or harmed by the fire?

3. After the fire, do you think the ecosystem returned to its natural state? Why or why not?

Ecosystem Change #2: Ocean Hunters

4. How did hunting otters change the interactions in the ocean ecosystem?

5. Which plants and animals were helped or harmed when people hunted the sea otters?

6. After the hunting had stopped, did the ecosystem return to its natural state? Why or why not?

Ecosystem Change #3: Something Is Fishy in Yellowstone Lake

7. How might adding lake trout to Yellowstone Lake change the interactions in the lake?

8. Which plants and animals were helped or harmed when someone added lake trout to Yellowstone Lake?

9. Do you think the ecosystem will return to its natural state? Why or why not?

Rachel Louise Carson

(1907–1964)

In the early to mid-1900s, there were few rules or laws about the environment. It was a time when many people thought that new pesticides (chemicals that killed insects) were the answer to insect problems. Insects killed trees in forests. Insects ruined food crops. In dairies, insects bothered cattle and dairy workers. The pesticides killed insects that spread disease and ruined crops. Many government, industry, and scientific authorities said that chemical pesticides were a great benefit to people. They claimed that chemical pesticides were perfectly safe. But were they really safe?

Rachel Carson wondered if all pesticides were safe, especially after reading a troubling letter from a friend. The letter explained that workers from the state government had sprayed the local salt marshes with DDT, a pesticide. They sprayed the DDT to kill the mosquitoes, but the wind had carried the DDT to other places. The pesticide had killed much more than mosquitoes in the salt marsh! Dr. Carson's friend found many dead birds, honeybees, and grasshoppers. The letter said that the mosquitoes were as bad as ever.

It also said that the government planned to spray again. Rachel Carson's friend asked for her help in getting scientists to call for a ban on the use of DDT.

Little was known about DDT and other insect-killing chemicals. Some scientists, including Rachel Carson, thought that more should be known about pesticides before they were sprayed in the environment. Dr. Carson had many questions about pesticides. She wondered how pesticides interacted with living things. She wanted to know how pesticides changed natural interactions. She was especially concerned about food webs. She wondered what effects pesticides had on living things, including people.

Why Was Rachel Carson Famous?

Until that time, Rachel Carson spent much of her life learning and writing about interactions in the sea. Her books described the underwater world so vividly that a person reading the books could almost see the interactions and feel the stormy tides. Now, upset by her friend's letter, Rachel Carson turned her attention away from the sea and toward pesticides. She wanted to learn as much as she could about them.

What Did Dr. Carson Learn?

She searched for evidence about how DDT changed interactions in the environment. She also searched for evidence about the effect DDT had on living things. She talked with many experts and other scientists. She read volumes of papers and books. The more Dr. Carson learned, the more alarmed she became.

Through her careful investigations, Dr. Carson found that spraying pesticides started a series of poisonings that harmed many living things. She found that when pesticides were sprayed over a salt marsh, the chemical landed on plankton, algae, and on nearby farm crops. The animals that ate those green plants for food also swallowed the pesticides. Animals that depended on other animals for food swallowed the pesticides as they ate the animals that had eaten the sprayed plants. Soon, all of the living things that were linked through the food web—plants, insects, fishes, shellfish, birds, raccoons, and people—had eaten the DDT. Rachel Carson also learned that the pesticides killed many helpful insects that served as natural pest controls. Without the natural insect controls, the numbers of harmful and bothersome insects increased.

Imagine a spring time when no birds sang, no grasshoppers hopped, no crickets chirped, and no bees buzzed. Imagine no flowers and no green grass. Imagine trees covered with brown, droopy leaves. Imagine dirty, brown streams and lakes. Imagine sick dogs, cats, cows, and horses—and some dead ones. Imagine sick and dying people. Imagine a spring with no sound. Imagine a deadly silence in the air.
—*Rachel Carson*, Silent Spring (1962)

Rachel Carson's book changed the course of history. Today many people are concerned about keeping the environment clean and safe. There are laws that regulate the use of dangerous chemicals. As a result of these laws, DDT and some other harmful chemicals are not used in this country.

However, they are allowed and used in other countries around the world. If everything is connected to everything else, what could the continued use of this and other pesticides in other countries mean?

Rachel Carson used her scientific knowledge, her writing talent, and her respect for nature to make people think about nature in a new way. She made people understand that we are as much a part of nature as other animals and plants. She made people understand that chemicals like pesticides must be used carefully because the future of all life depends upon the actions and decisions made by people.

Part A: Read and discuss the following statement with your teammates. Then talk about the questions. Write your own response to each question in your notebook. Be prepared to share your responses with the class.

All plants and animals, including humans, cause changes in the environments where they live. Some of the changes are harmful and some are helpful.

1. What change has happened in your neighborhood or town? Describe the change and tell what (or who) caused it.

2. Was the change helpful, harmful, or both? Describe what (or who) was helped or harmed by the change and why you think so.

Part B: Review the "Doing Science" section on pages 1–19. Look at the graphic organizer on page 2. Talk about ways that you were doing science during this lesson. Then, on your own, describe ways in which you were doing science in your notebook.

Part C: Think about the activities that you did and the strategies that you used during this lesson. Talk about the following questions with your teammates. Then write your own response to each question in your notebook.

1. What did you learn during this lesson?

2. What activities or strategies helped you learn? How or why were they helpful?

3. Did working as a team help you learn? Why or why not?

4. What skills did your team do well? What skills does your team need to improve?

 Lesson 9

Creating Your Own Ecosystem

What have you learned about interactions and ecosystems? Do you know more about the interactions within ecosystems than you did in lesson 1? It's time to find out!

On Your Own

Creatures and Creations

In lesson 1, you chose a ticket for a video adventure and visited an ecosystem on film. Since then, you have observed your own study systems and studied many more types of ecosystems. In lesson 9, you will choose one imaginary creature and learn about it from its characteristics and written description. You will need to determine an existing ecosystem or create your own ecosystem for this organism. You can be as creative as you like!

Through a project of your choice, you will become an expert on this creature and its ecosystem. You can create a diorama, a poster, a book, a travel guide, a song, or a story to explain the interactions of this creature with living and nonliving things. You also will show or write about the interactions between other living things and nonliving things in this ecosystem. And when your project is complete, you will attend an annual ecological institute to present your findings. Other scientists (classmates) will present their projects and attend this institute.

Your Task

Create or find an ecosystem for an imaginary creature. Use your notebook records, resource materials, and what you have learned in this module to help you do a project of your choice. Present this project at the annual ecological institute in your classroom.

Directions follow for this project. Your teacher also has a rubric that will help you make sure you have completed everything you need to do.

Your Supplies

- glue

- 1 pair of scissors

- 1 sheet of poster board (if needed)

- 1 copy of "Homeless Creatures"

- 1 copy of "Ecosystem Project Rubric"

- your notebook

- art supplies

- markers, colored pencils, or crayons

- 1 pencil

Directions

1. Meet with others who have the same imaginary creature, talk about possible ecosystems, and review your notebook records for ideas.

    a. What kinds of living things might be found in this creature's ecosystem?

    b. What kinds of nonliving things might be found in this creature's ecosystem?

    c. What kinds of interactions might happen in this creature's ecosystem?

2. Decide what new information you need to do your project. Record a list of questions you want to answer.

    a. Are there other plants and animals that live in the ecosystem? If creating an ecosystem, what kinds of plants and animals might live in the ecosystem?

    b. What do the animals use for food? How do they get their food?

    c. How do the plants meet their needs?

d. What are the climate and weather like? Are they the same all year or do they change with the seasons?

e. What is the soil like? Is it dark, rich soil? Is it sandy? Is it heavy clay? Is it rocky?

f. Is there plenty of water or little water in this ecosystem? What kind of water is available?

g. What are the land features like? Is the land flat? Are there hills? Are there mountains?

3. Find resource materials that can help you answer your questions or give you ideas for your own ecosystem.

4. After you have gathered enough information about the ecosystem, start your project. Your project should include something about the following things. Check the rubric for more details.

a. The role of the Sun in the ecosystem

b. A food web that identifies the producers, consumers, and decomposers

Use your notebook records to help you remember all the things you can describe about an ecosystem.

c. A description of the interactions between the living and nonliving things (how the plants and animals depend on one another and on nonliving things to survive)

d. A description of what it would be like to live there (what you might see, what the weather would be like, what might change during the seasons)

e. A way to show the connections between the living and nonliving things

f. A description of how the living things meet their needs to survive

g. Why these living things live in this kind of ecosystem and not somewhere else

5. Prepare a presentation of your project for the ecological institute to be held in your classroom.

✓ Checking Understanding

Part A: Talk about the following questions with your teammates. Then write your own response to each question in your notebook. Be prepared to share your responses with the class.

1. What did you learn about ecosystems that you didn't know before?

2. What did you like best about learning about ecosystems?

3. What two questions do you have about the ecosystem in which you live?

4. What two questions do you want to answer about ecosystems in general? (What do you wonder about ecosystems?)

Part B: Review the "Doing Science" section on pages 1–19. Look at the graphic organizer on page 2. Talk about ways that you were doing science during this lesson. Then, on your own, describe ways in which you were doing science in your notebook.

Part C: Think about the activities that you did and the strategies that you used during this lesson. Talk about the following questions with your teammates. Then write your own response to each question in your notebook.

1. What did you learn during this lesson?

2. What activities or strategies helped you learn? How or why were they helpful?

3. Did working as a team help you learn? Why or why not?

4. What skills did your team do well? What skills does your team need to improve?

Glossary

axis: A horizontal or vertical line in a graph on which we write numbers or labels.

brainstorm: A skill that teams use to think of a list of ideas before beginning an investigation or solving a problem.

consumer: An organism that uses food, other living things, made by a producer.

coring: Drilling a hole in a tree to remove a piece of wood to examine tree growth rings.

data: Information collected in a scientific investigation.

decomposer: An organism that breaks down dead plants and animals and returns them to soil.

drought: A long period of time with very little or no rain.

ecologist: A scientist who studies interactions between living and nonliving things in all kinds of places.

ecosystem: All living and nonliving things in a given area that interact with one another.

food chain: A diagram of the organisms according to the order in which each organism uses the next as a food source.

food web: A diagram of overlapping food chains.

interact: To act upon one another.

materials manager: Has the team job of getting the supplies that are listed in the "Team Supplies" section for each lesson; when the team task is completed, the materials manager returns the supplies to the supply table.

messenger: Has the team job to ask another team's messenger or your teacher for help if the team gets stuck.

plankton: Very small plants and animals that live in water.

producer: Organisms that can make their own food.

record: A writing, drawing, chart, or graph.

skill builder: Has the job of encouraging teammates to practice the team skills.

tracker: Has the team job of keeping track of what the team is doing and makes sure the team does every step and follows the directions in order.

zero point: The point where the horizontal and vertical lines on a graph meet; where the graph begins.

Acknowledgments

Photo Credits

Allen Young, Milwaukee Public Museum: p. 98; p. 99; p. 100; p. 104

Cameron Davidson - SERC: p. 30, p. 31; p. 108; p. 110; p. 112; p. 114; p. 115

Carlye Calvin: p. 65 (top right); p. 65 (bottom left); p. 81; p. 123; p. 126; p. 127 (top left); p. 127 (top right); p. 127 (bottom left); p. 127 (bottom right); p. 128; p. 129; p. 157; p. 159; p. 160; p. 192

Charles Newman/Visuals Unlimited: p. 182

Comstock: p. 8 (right); p. 29

Corbis: p. 9 (right)

Corbis-Bettman: p. 200; p. 203

Corel: p. 37; p. 52 (bottom); p. 82; p. 84; p. 91; p. 155; p. 156; p. 145; p. 147

Daniel D. Lamorequx/Visuals Unlimited: p. 181

Digital Stock: p. 19

Dreamstime/Terry Ryder; p. 183

Dreamstime/Yali Shi; p. 87

Eyewire: p. 51; p. 67; p. 161; p. 187

Glenn M. Oliver/Visuals Unlimited: p. 191

iStockphoto: p. 4 (left); p. 5 (right); p. 6 (left); p. 8 (left); p. 9 (left); p. 16; p. 49; p. 50; p. 52 (top); p. 53 (far left); p. 53 (2nd from left); p. 53 (far right); p. 72; p. 85; p. 86; p. 88; p. 90; p. 92; p. 93; p. 188; p. 189

Text Credits

Cover Credits